A PRIVATE EYE'S GUIDE TO

COLLECTING A BAD DEBT

Creighton-Morgan Publishing Group
P.O. Box 470862, San Francisco CA   94147-0862
(415)   922-6684

A Private Eye's Guide to Collecting a Bad Debt

Fay Faron

Published by:
Creighton-Morgan Publishing Group
P.O. Box 470862, San Francisco Ca 94147-0862
Publisher's Cataloging in Publication
(Prepared by Quality Books Inc.)

Faron, Fay, 1949-
  A private eye's guide to collecting a bad debt / Fay Faron. --
  p. cm.
  ISBN 0-9620096-7-9

  1. Collecting of accounts--Handbooks, manuals, etc. 2.
Collection agents. 3. Private investigators. I. Title.

HG3752.7.U6   346.077
                         QBI91-501

Printed in the United States of America
ISBN 0-9620096-7-9

Look What They're Saying

"It's the book that proves there is something you can do about getting ripped off and screwed over!" **Lee Rodgers, KGO-Radio, San Francisco, CA**

"A wonderful reference book! Excellent reading for anyone working with fugitives or white collar crime." **Chuck Latting, Special Agent, FBI, San Francisco**

"Dear Rat Dog, Bought your book and read it. Then I read it again and again. Great entertainment! But better than that, it works!" **Charles E. McCall, Judgment Creditor, Oakdale, CA**

"A Private Eye's Guide to Collecting a Bad Debt should be required reading for every new, and even seasoned police officer." **Stoney Brook, Criminal Inspector, District Attorney's Office, Santa Cruz, CA**

"More than just another how to book. It's pure inspiration with a dab of genius and a touch of humor." **Hunter International Books**

"But listen, Faron's book is something else. She has a rare talent. Nothing is so needed as humor in business, and obviously she is able to do a magnificent job of it." **Betty Spickard, "Prunella-Tittletop", Ozarks Mountaineer, Springfield, MO**

"This unique book is alive with ideas for adaptation and promotion. The possibilities would have me dancing!" **Ernestine Gilbreth Carey, Author, Cheaper by the Dozen, Phoenix, AZ**

iii

"The great surprise about this book is that it's fun to read!" **Bob Mackowiak, P.I. Magazine**

"A masterful effort and a 'must-have' addition to the library of every private investigator..." **Dick Hickman, California Ass'n of Licensed Investigators**

"An invaluable source for the judgment-creditor, done with an even more invaluable sense of humor." **Stan Pierce, Marin County Small Claims Advisor**

"Suddenly after ten years, a man I couldn't even find, now is making frantic phone calls to me. It's amazing what a little 'ratdogging' will do." **Donna Warren, 'The Ex-wife from Hell', San Jose CA**

"It has been a long time since I have had so much fun reading a reference book - and reference is my business!" **Bob Davidsson, Librarian, South Florida**

"Terrific, amusing, well written & useful. I can't wait until someone stiffs me so I can try it out." **Ed Hooks, Acting Coach, San Francisco CA**

"I am just so glad there is a 'Joan of Arc' for us 'small' victims of this pain in the @#! paper chase." **David Salomon, Landlord, San Francisco CA**

"A good, accessible book for those who want to try it themselves before hiring a dick to track down a rat." **George Hampton, Booklist**

"This is the best book written on any subject, in any language, by anyone, anywhere in the world." **Mother of the Author.**

About The Author

S/W/F Non-vegetarian. Non-smoker. Is single but has had offers. Prefers soaps over P.B.S., trash over classics, twinkies over fiber. Enjoys shoot-outs, stake-outs, disguises and fast get-aways.

Dedication

To Rick, Kevin, Cindy, Jerry and Al, whose support has always been absolute.

Thanks To

Ken Milburn. For his computer, patience and companionship.

David Pope. For his publishing expertise, and his unselfish sharing of it.

Stan Burford. For finding my first 60 pages when his computer ate them. And for his wit, warmth, and years of friendship.

Jerry Faron & Rick Tierney. Whose editing made me look smart.

Larry Plotkin. For being the only guy I know who can tell a Grantee from a Grantor. And for settling for my undying devotion, when he could have had cash.

Al Brito. For lunch.

A PRIVATE EYE'S GUIDE TO COLLECTING A BAD DEBT

But First

Okay. Let's cut the suspense. Let's talk about why I call myself Rat Dog Dick.

When I was born, I was a very ugly little mousepuppy. I was premature, bald and wrinkly. Mom took one look at me and yelled, "Rats! What a pooch! Dick, get over here and see what you've done!"

Actually, I just made that up.

What really happened was, sometime after I was born I bought a houseboat in Sausalito, just across the bridge from San Francisco. Six weeks later it sank. This happened during the big Christmas storm of 1982 when most of Northern California ended up in Southern California.

After the phone started working again, I called the man who sold me the boat and asked for my money back. I figured I was entitled. After all, the boat had listed badly before it sank, which practically screams water in the hull. I quoted the law of disclosure and a lot of other ten-letter words.

"Ha, ha," he said. I could just see him twirling his handle bar mustache as he spoke. He was obviously a great fan of the old buyer-beware adage. And so, I did what any red blooded American would do. I sued.

But in order to win the suit, I had to prove there was water in the hull. And to do that, I had to find the guy who had rented the boat for the last two years and convince him to testify that the boat listed more and more throughout the years.

The prognosis was grim. The guy was a recluse. All I could find out about him was that he was a 300 pound Breatharian who played the sitar. God knows how many of those there were in Marin.

Despite the odds, just two days later I tracked him down. He had changed his name to a mantra and gone off to live in a cave in Texas.

Hey, just a lucky hunch.

My attorney was impressed. So impressed, in fact, that he hired me to find three people for him. "There are three people who owe me money," he said. "If you find them, and you find the money, I'll give you half."

I was a freelance TV producer at the time, which was synonymous with being unemployed, so I gave it a shot.

First I went down to the library where you can get books on how to do everything, and I looked for a book on how to find money, but I couldn't find one. I tried bookstores. No luck. I even subscribed to those weird catalogues that tell you how to make bombs and bury family members in your own back yard, but even they didn't have any books on how to collect money. (I've since found out that burying members of your family in your own back yard is pretty tame stuff compared to finding money.)

And so, since I couldn't find a book on collecting money, I made most of it up as I went along.

And I learned a lot. I had always heard that a lot of really embarrassing and intimate stuff is right there in the public records, just for the looking. So I tried it. I went to the County Clerk's Office and looked through the index of their files. I went to the County Recorder's Office and did the same. Then Voter's Registration, Traffic Court, Divorce Court, etc., etc., etc. Within a week I found my attorney's three scoundrels, and I was beginning to learn a lot about where they kept their money.

It wasn't long until I was hooked. Yes, it's true. I became a public access junkie!

It all started innocently enough. At first I'd just stop off in the county courthouse each morning before going to work. I would be late, of course, but my boss bought the old dead grandma story, no sweat.

But soon I found that pre-breakfast snooping wasn't enough. I'd try to sneak a quick peek in during my lunch break, or knock off early to get in a little sleuthing before closing time.

Then it became an obsession. I found I could no longer go out on a date without running a credit check. At parties, I could always be found out in my car simulating a stake-out. Eventually I was even detained for checking out "comfort stops" in a Pacific Height's back yard.

Eventually, I hit bottom. My obsession led to less and less TV work. I didn't care. "TV is for Pooh Bears!" was my battle cry.

Meanwhile, my skip-tracing business was thriving. My attorney recommended me to other attorneys. "This little lady can find money like a rat dog finds rats," he said, and the name stuck.

September rolled around and Rat Dog Dick got listed in the yellow pages. People called up just to find out if I was real, and soon the media climbed on board. Before long, the name of Rat Dog Dick was known far and wide as the skip-tracer who could find people like a rat dog finds rats.

This made a lot of real-live detectives very nervous. A lot of detectives don't like other detectives very much anyway, and they like little blonde girls who run around being unlicensed detectives even less.

I wasn't a detective-trainee, I claimed, but a "skip-tracer." A skip-tracer is a person who tracks down scoundrels using only public records. The state of California doesn't mind if you do this without a license as long as you never talk to anyone. Of course, it is very difficult to do this without ever opening your mouth and they know it. That is why you meet so few deaf mute skip-tracers.

The difference between a skip-tracer and a detective is that while a skip-tracer must limit his activities to scouring the volumes of public access, a detective can do this, plus interview people, lie to them (and their mothers), have occasional shoot-outs, repossess cars at will, and freely break into places without the nagging threat of arrest. (Well, not really.)

I was merrily pursuing my career as skip-tracer when one day the phone rang. A "client" called, asking me to track down his 15-year old daughter who, he said, his wife had wrongly taken from him in their divorce proceedings. He asked how I worked. I said public access. He said, "That won't work in this case, because she is only 15-years old and there won't be any paper on her."

Aha! I said. In that case, I'd probably do something like go talk to the neighbors.

Well, dum de dum dum, I'm in big trouble now.

The "client" on the phone turned out to be no client at all, but a representative of the Department of Consumer Affairs. They had caught me red-handed at being a detective without a license! I got a letter saying to cease and desist and a whole lot more. They suggested, strongly I might add, that I apply for my private investigator's license. I did and was dumbstruck when I found that my years of television investigative reporting, plus all that skip-tracing had qualified me to take the test.

There were a hundred questions, multiple choice, some very hard, and some like "What is Perry Mason's detective's name?" and "What year did Dick Tracy first appear in the comic strips?" Anyway, they happened to ask a lot of stuff I knew about. Stuff about rigor mortis. Stuff about following people. Stuff I'd seen on TV or read about in books. Some stuff I had even learned on the job.

I passed the test and became a full-fledged and fully licensed private investigator, operating under the name of the Rat Dog Dick Detective Agency in San Francisco. And that's how I came to be Rat Dog Dick, the detective who finds money like a rat dog finds rats.

1

Portrait of a Scoundrel

Okay. Get this.

It's a foggy night. Cat paws and all that. You know, August in the City.

Out steps Rat Dog.

"There are two kinds of people in this world," says Rat Dog, "Scoundrels, and seekers of scoundrels." She lights a cigarette, pulls her trench coat tight against her mauve tear-gas gun, and saunters on.

Scoundrels aren't mean, claims Rat Dog. Just ornery. "They just don't like having to pay for stuff."

That's where Rat Dog Dick comes in. If your scoundrel has made off with the loot, for $150, Rat Dog will find 'em for you. For two hundred, she'll date him and dump him.

It's a dirty job, but somebody's got to do it.

1

It always begins the same.

For a time everything goes fine in your business dealings.

Then come the signs. Your phone calls aren't being returned. The payments are late. Checks start bouncing. You call and the phone is disconnected. (They probably forgot to pay the phone bill, you reason.) You go there and the office is deserted. (Probably thieves in the night.) There's no forwarding address on file. (It's that darn post office again.)

Eventually, you begin to suspect the worst. The guy's a scoundrel.

You push your suspicions aside. You don't want to believe it, but the situation is beginning to get on your nerves. And besides, you're just plain getting mad!

By now, you're desperate to get the guy's attention. So you decide to sue. You don't even think it will get to court. You figure the shock of being served will shame him into action. You have a hard time serving him, of course, because you can't find him. But eventually you do. Surely now he'll call. He knows you mean business.

But he doesn't call. You figure he's embarrassed. Maybe he's had some financial reversals. Well, he can tell it to the judge.

He's embarrassed all right. So gosh darned embarrassed, in fact, that he fails to show up in court. You win by default.

Of course, you expect him to mail you a check immediately. Obviously he's seen the error of his ways. After all, the judge agrees that he owes you money.

You wait a week. Two weeks. A month.

No check.

Eventually you go looking for the guy. But he's gone.

2

Boy was he embarrassed!

Wrong!!!

You've just been suckered by a scoundrel! There are no statistics, but I suspect it happens once in the life of every man, good and true.

And so there you are, armed with the full power of the court. You have a "judgment" and everybody agrees that he owes you the money. Yet no one is demanding that he pay up. Where do you go from here?

No, the court will not set up a payment plan. No, they won't throw him in jail if he doesn't pay. No, they won't even send him a second notice. Yes, Scarlett, it's true. They just don't give a damn!

Every self-respecting scoundrel knows that there is no punishment for non-payment of debt. Debtors prison went out with Dickens. Sure they add interest. So what? He's not going to pay you anyway!

The truth is, all the court can do is to legally declare that you are owed money. Later they will provide you with the court order that you will need in order to collect it. But locating the money is your responsibility. They simply cannot know where someone's assets are. It's a huge job and, too often, unrewarding.

So it is up to the judgment-creditor to fill that gap between being awarded a judgment and what we in the detective biz call "getting the money."

And you can bet your little brother, if your scoundrel didn't show up in court, he knows something you don't. He's judgment-proof.

WHAT IS JUDGMENT-PROOF?

Judgment-proof means that your scoundrel has protected himself against the kind of legal steps that you must take in order to collect from him.

Maybe he owns his own home. But can you get it? Probably not. In most states, a primary residence cannot be sold to satisfy a debt other than the mortgage. As an added safeguard, the property might even be homesteaded. Or in someone else's name.

So you go after the car. Foiled again! In most states a car cannot be attached if it is used for work. In others, there must be a certain amount of equity in the vehicle.

But don't give up. I can and have collected money from people like this. Not always. But often.

More times than not, these guys slip up. If you're persistent, quick on follow-through, and you never ever give up, you can take their money away from them against their will.

Here's how... .

2

Can You Collect?

Attorneys: Are unpaid legal fees the reason that Mercedes dealers snicker when you walk through the door?

Landlords: When you asked for first and last, did you forget to mention that you'd like to be paid for the months in between?

Mothers: When he whispered sweet nothings, how could you know he was referring to child support?

It sounds like a case for Rat Dog Dick, the detective who finds people like a rat dog finds rats

I know you're anxious to get started. You've seen yourself defined in Chapter One, and you know in your heart of hearts that you've been "suckered by

5

a scoundrel."

Alright, let's not mince words. It's embarrassing! Millions of people will read this book. They'll
remember you, and that story you told them and
they'll be laughing behind your back. "Ha. Ha. Ha,"
they'll be saying. "You remember Poor George, don't
you? You know, the guy who got suckered by a
scoundrel? Ha. Ha. Ha." Let's face it. This probably
isn't what you'd hoped for on your epitaph.

Not to worry. No need to attend any more
Suckers Anonymous meetings, join the victim reloca-
tion program, change your name, get extensive plas-
tic surgery or move to another city. No need to
continue to be the butt of tasteless jokes at the
company Christmas party. Relief is on the way! Now
that you have admitted that you're a sucker, you can
begin to remedy the situation.

First, find condolence in numbers. Statistics
show only 25% of single parents collect their full
support, and 50% collect no support at all. That adds
up to *nine billion dollars* owed nationwide! And that's
just child support. There are millions of landlords,
plenty of entrepreneurs, lawyers, and just plain really
smart guys who've been suckered by a scoundrel.

So first, you're not alone. And secondly, you
know now that there is a chance that you can get your
money back. No guarantees. But a chance.

Oh, I can hear you saying, "C'mon, I bought the
book! How come I still might not get my money back?"

Brace yourself, my friend. It's not because I
didn't write a good enough book. It's because the
courts are against you. Americans have been railing
for years against the lenient treatment of dangerous
criminals in this country. Prisons are so full that life
imprisonment now routinely means ten to fifteen
years. Guys with just a few homicides under their

belts get out early to make room for newcomers.

It's the same for scoundrels. The courts don't have the time nor inclination to deal with them. Not that scoundrels go to jail, they don't. Scoundrels are charged with civil crimes, not criminal crimes. And civil crimes are not punishable by incarceration.

So, can you send your scoundrel to jail if you want to? Maybe. Read on.

SCOUNDREL OR CRIMINAL?

You have two options when you prepare to sue. You can sue in Small Claims, Municipal or Superior Court and get a money judgment, or you go to the District Attorney and initiate criminal charges.

Most people opt to bring civil charges against their nemesis. Why? One, because they don't normally think in terms of criminal charges, and if they do, usually their revenge does not extend to forcing incarceration upon someone. In short, they just want their money back. Unfortunately, it's not that simple.

I hate to be the one to tell you this, but you've got the Great American System working against you. Just as the law protects the criminal, innocent until proven guilty and all that, the law also protects the scoundrel.

Everyone is suit-happy in this country, and that's probably the basis of the problem. The courts are leaning over backwards to protect the defendant.

First off, judgments are largely unenforceable. If you've got one, check it out. What does it say? That you are owed money. When is it due? Doesn't say. What are the terms? Doesn't say. What are the penalties if it's never paid? Doesn't say.

What then is a judgment? It's a trophy. A nice little something to hang on your wall next to your

7

diplomas to prove that, yes indeed, you were right in a civil dispute. Not exactly what you'd hoped for wehn you spent all that money on attorney's fees.

Okay, so you accept the fact that you will have to take an active part in the recovery of the funds. The court will issue you a subpoena, an order of examination, a writ of attachment and wage garnishment. Yippee. But the court will do even more for the defendant. It will protect his home against attachment. It will protect his car, tools of his trade and most of his personal property from being sold to satisfy your debt. It will not prosecute or even pursue him, if he ignores the obligation and moves to another state. He can list his real estate under another name, change his bank account daily and protect his income from garnishment. And all of it is legal. He can even end the harassment by having the judgment vacated, as if the suit never took place!

So you see, it's not my fault if you can't collect. It's the court's. But I will tell you everything you can possibly do in order to get your money. If it can be gotten, this book will show you how to get it.

At one point, while writing this book, I almost quit. I was so discouraged about the lack of support from the court system, that I felt dishonest writing a book on how to collect money when a lot of it was simply uncollectable. But I kept going. Because a lot of it *is* collectible. And because you won't know until you try. And because you have the right to pursue your judgment. You have the right to collect it or to know beyond a shadow of a doubt that you can't.

And that's what I suggest. Read the book. Do everything you can to get the money. Be aggressive and obnoxious and a righteous pain in the bum. Get what money you can. And when you're done, close the book and get on with your life.

8

SO TELL ME ABOUT CRIMINAL CHARGES

What kinds of cases will the district attorney prosecute? In short, the deciding factor is whether there was criminal intent on the part of the scoundrel. The D.A. usually considers two things in determining whether to bring criminal charges against someone. Criminal intent, and the number of victims involved. Is this a scam he has pulled repeatedly? If there are other victims, the D.A. just might handle your case.

And what if the D.A. does agree to take the case? What does that mean to you?

First, initiating criminal charges is a very strong incentive for the scoundrel to pay up. Most hard-core scoundrels are pretty nonchalant about having civil charges filed against them. They know how difficult judgments are to collect. Many times, they ignore the suit altogether and don't even show up in court to defend themselves. But criminal charges? That's different! Now, we're talking jail! You know jail. Small rooms. Bad food. Very little time in the exercise yard. So that's one reason for considering initiating a criminal rather than a civil suit.

And what about collection? Is there any more assurance that you will get your money if you go for a criminal verdict? Not really. Remember the first rule of collections: *You can't get blood from a turnip.* And, once he's in the slammer, chances are his career will take a real nose dive. After all, it's tough to attach the wages of a guy who makes license plates for a living.

SIBERIAN SCOUNDREL

About the time I began writing this book, a man in Palo Alto California was awarded a judgment against

9

the Soviet Union. The California Supreme Court agreed with him that the Russians had slandered him by branding him a spy. Talk about assets! The vodka alone would knock you on your ear. Ironically, the only thing the man ever collected was a typewriter out of the Russian Trade Office in Washington D.C.

I was anxious to take the case, but I'd already committed myself to six months abroad on another assignment.

My plan was to slap a "For Sale" sign on the lawn of the San Francisco consulate. After all, a consulate is considered to be foreign soil! It might not have worked, but at least I would have gone down in history as the P.I. who started World War III.

A little publicity never hurts.

THE SIX KINDS OF SCOUNDRELS

Okay, I know I should have twelve. One for each astrological sign. You know, Pisces, the wishy-washy scoundrel, and all that. But I'm afraid I'm not up on my astrological risings. What I am up on, unfortunately, is scoundrels.

THE ACCIDENTAL SCOUNDREL

This is the lowest grade of scoundrel. This could be any one of us, and probably has been.

You're in the grocery store and the clerk rings in your $10.50 leg of lamb at $1.50. Do you tell him?

Or - you're riding behind a Brinks truck. Nobody's around. The doors fly open. Out falls a bag of money.

You grab the loot and try to catch up with the truck. It's gone, of course. And there just doesn't seem to be a pay phone anywhere. When finally you do find a pay phone, it's inconvenient to park. Besides, what if you go to all the trouble of parking, and then the phone is out of order? You can't leave all that money in your car while you deal with an out of order phone. Better not take the chance.

You head for home (or the Bahamas). You've got a lot on your mind, and you forget about the loot. When it does cross your thoughts, you, like Scarlett, vow to think about it tomorrow. What's to remind you? They'll announce it on TV. Put it in the papers. Maybe offer a reward.

But they don't. Maybe *they* forgot. Maybe they didn't notice. Maybe the Brinks driver was too embarrassed to tell his boss, and you're doing him a favor by keeping the money! He could lose his job, after all.

Time flies. It would look really bad to return the money now. Obviously, they don't want it, or they would have tracked *you* down, right? Besides, you're due some reward money.

Yeah, but the whole thing!

This kind of scoundrel pays when confronted. Trouble is, he doesn't do the "crime" unless there's a good chance he can get away with it. If he is caught, he'll blame it on forgetfulness or a simple mistake.

THE CIRCUMSTANTIAL SCOUNDREL

Circumstances have a lot to do with how most scoundrels get started.

Way back in kindergarten, most of us learned the ugly truth. We weren't the smartest kid in class. We weren't the prettiest. But, joy of joys, only in

11

America, can a kid grow up to be the richest!

That's the thing about rich. It doesn't take smarts (or so our little minds thought.) Look at that cowboy on the 6:00 news who won the lottery! All we need is one lucky break, and we can retire by 40! (Besides, *secretly*, we knew we were smarter than the next guy - street smarts - and street smarts don't show up on a geometry test!)

Then, still in high school, we get our first real job, slinging hamburgers, loving it, and making more money than we ever dreamed. By the time we graduate, we're on a first name basis with MasterCard.

Well, obviously, we have a gift. Life is easy, so why all the flack from Mom and Dad?

We write Visa and they right back. Now we're not limited to stretching that $3.24 an hour to cover our growing needs. A thousand dollar credit limit is like having a grand in the bank. Right?

But not for long. Suddenly, the credit limit's gone, turned into furniture for the new apartment, and Visa's not as friendly when they call. And those fifty dollar payments they claim they *need* are just like throwing money away! I mean, do you know what you could do with that fifty bucks if that mean Mr. MasterCard wasn't hounding you all the time?

Face it, my friend. You've become a circumstantial scoundrel.

Sure, if all of us had all the money we wanted, we'd pay our bills. But we don't. Trouble is, we still want all the *stuff*. So, what we do is - we *get* all the stuff, and then we tap dance on the telephone, paying everybody a little something so nobody gets too mad.

It's a stage most of us go through, and if we're lucky we learn, and monitor our own behavior before the courts - and sometimes the law - monitors it for us.

If this is the sort of scoundrel you have, dance

with him. But let your drum beat a little louder than the next guy, and there's a good chance you'll get paid. Unless, of course, he turns into....

THE BIG FALL SCOUNDREL

The Big Fall Scoundrel looks like a good credit risk. He drives a nice car, lives in a nice house. Has a pretty wife. Has made it big in the business world.

This scoundrel has had money so long, he thinks it's his due and can conceive of life no other way. A lot of times The Big Fall Scoundrel hit it big right out of college. In today's economy, many of them are in real estate related fields - contracting, mortgage lending, selling, and so forth. When prices went up and up, investing in real estate was a sure thing. Every year - in this neck of the woods, at least - people made an easy 20% to 30% return on their investments. And when that investment was a $50,000 to $100,000 house, their portfolios grew by leaps and bounds.

But that was then, and this is now. As of this writing, real estate isn't skyrocketing, and it may never do so again. That leaves a lot of these whiz-kid financiers holding the bag. Trouble is, they can't adjust. Being rich is what they *do*, and it takes a long time to realize that. And their creditors are the last to know.

But sometimes it is more than a sluggish economy that brings The Big Fall Scoundrel to his knees. Personal tragedy plays a part in many cases. Sometimes, it's a divorce. Sometimes, an automobile accident. Sometimes, alcohol or drug abuse.

Again, the achilles heel of The Big Fall Scoundrel, is that he thinks he is above being reduced to the

13

common man and rarely, if ever, realizes what is happening to him before it's too late. He thinks he can absorb this setback, and the bucks are going to keep rolling in. He thinks he can get rid of that hag of a wife, give her a little something to go away, and finally get that fine young thing at the office. He thinks he can anesthetize his fears with booze or drugs, and exude the old confidence that will again convince people to buy his product.

Meanwhile, all the time he's sliding down toward ranch house living, he still *looks* rich. He still drives the car. Still has the phone in the car. Still goes to lunch at Vanessi's. And this is why he is lulled into thinking this too will pass. Because he still has all the *stuff!*

The Big Fall Scoundrel is one of the most treacherous. That's because by the time the check he gave you bounces, a whole lot of others have bounced too. You know, the old get in line syndrome. Many times, this is the scoundrel who brings you to your knees. The others you can reason with, but The Big Fall Scoundrel can't help you because he has absolutely no idea how *not* to be rich.

THE THIRD NOTICE SCOUNDREL

This scoundrel is basically good at heart, they're just The Circumstantial Scoundrel dug in a little deeper.

I once had a partner - heck of a good sport she was - who was a Third Notice Scoundrel. We started a business and it didn't quite fly. We paid our bills, but we just couldn't pay every bill every month. Cindy put them in chronological order, and when some income came in, she plucked the first one off the pile and paid it.

14

Things got a little worse. Soon these bills weren't arriving in black ink, they were written in red. When a creditor called, Cindy's response was to ask indignantly, "Well, have you sent us a *final* notice?"

The best way to deal with these scoundrels is to coax your money out of them and then put them on a C.O.D. basis. Don't be surprised if they take their business elsewhere. After all, their supplier of choice is the guy who will extend credit.

THE SUBPOENA SCOUNDREL

Same thing, one grade below. This scoundrel has too many red notices to pay them all. He only pays bills that come attached to a summons.

Deal with him the way you handled The Third Notice Scoundrel.

THE HIDE & SEEK SCOUNDREL

I hate this one! They drive me nuts. They lie, lie, lie and they think you're buying it!

I once had a client, whom I'll call Robert Whalen, who bugged me until I agreed to follow his wife, Dolores. That made me mad to begin with, because I personally think people should be allowed to do whatever they want. If you're wife's cheating on you, then in my book, you need a marriage counselor, not a detective.

But anyway, Whalen finally guilted me into it. He evoked our old "friendship" - which meant that we had once worked in the same building. I recommended another private investigator, but that guy wanted a retainer, so Whalen came back to me.

15

Nobody but me could help him, he pleaded. And of course, she was due to cheat on him tomorrow, so there was no time to get me any money.

My first clue should have been that he never mentioned money at all. I mentioned it, of course, said I wouldn't do this for my best friend, (sitting in a parked car all day is a total bummer) and in fact, my best friend wouldn't ask me. Nobody who really cared about me would ask me to sit in a parked car all day long and watch a building. None of this fazed Whalen.

Anyway, I did it. (She was good as gold. The guy who she was supposedly cheating with, however, went to lunch with someone else, and spent an hour in the back seat of his car with the little lady. I have some fine shots of this, if you're interested.)

That week no money arrived, and the next Wednesday morning Robert Whalen called again.

I had to go again, he insisted. (She, according to him, only cheats on Wednesdays.) Ooops! Forgot to mail the check. Well he'll get me "something" this week. No asking about how much this was costing, what the bill was, what I charged per hour, etc. He was too desperate to think of any of that now.

Again, the wife was cheating free.

Whalen called during the week and I made it clear to him I wasn't following his wife a third time, until he paid his bill. He said, okay, he'd send it, but he never asked how much it was.

When Whalen called the next Wednesday at 6:30 a.m., he was frantic. He hadn't had a chance to get the check in the mail, but he was just sure his wife would be cheating that day! I had to help him. He was getting ready "to make his move."

Sorry, Whalen, if she's really an adulteress, then she'll still be doing it next Wednesday. You know next Wednesday, don't you? It's the Wednesday *after you pay your bill!* Whalen said he could get me "something" by the fifteenth.

It was a month later - and after a nasty letter, that I next heard from Robert Whalen. He left a message on my machine that said, sorry, misunderstanding. Not February 15th, March 15th was when he could pay "something."

Well, March 15th came and went and so did the case in small claims court. Robert Whalen didn't show up, and so after enduring a dirty look from the judge (he didn't seem to think Whalen's marital problems were any of my business either) I got a default judgment.

One whole Robert Whalen year-free later, I finally got around to collecting. I attached his wages, and only then did I hear from him.

Oh yeah, he'd forgotten all about it. He really wanted to pay, but he was being laid off from his job (according to his boss, he quit) and he was declaring bankruptcy. The only reason he was holding off on bankruptcy was so he could pay this off first!

Immediately he quit his job, and was left again to track down a place of employment. So far, I have spent three times as much time investigating my former client as I did investigating his wife.

But I know some good stuff. I know, for example, that Whalen was collecting unemployment while he working at the job where I attached his wages.

His license plate and the vehicle identification number on his car don't match. The VIN number comes back to him, but it shows another plate - and so many parking tickets that he was unable to reregister his car. The plate on Whalen's car belonged to a man who reported it stolen six months before.

Whalen also sent me a $25 check once (it never cleared) in an envelope marked with a postage meter dated six months before. I tracked the number down to an old employer of Whalen's. He even ran postage off on a bunch of envelopes for his personal use before he left the company!

The upshot of this is that I am still collecting from Robert Whalen. Every time he changes jobs, it costs me $20 to reopen the sheriff's file, and that money, and the interest, is added to Whalen's judgment.

Whalen, if you are reading this - or your wife, who by now has received a copy of this book in the mail - you will never be free of me until you *pay your bill!*

I mean it.

THE OUT & OUT CON-MAN

The Out & Out Con-Man is the guy who ends up on *Geraldo!* He's the one who get's all the press - the guy with 109 wives. The lady who killed three husbands for the insurance money. The sociopath most of us know to stay away from.

Most of the pictures you see of The Out & Out Con-Man are still photos, taken just before he split town. The reason you rarely see any footage of these folks is because they are moving faster than the speed of light. And what you don't get from seeing those still photos, is that The Out & Out Con Man looks just like everybody else. He's got that face that gets lost in a crowd.

Which is exactly why he gets away with this. Because we expect him to look like Mark Harmon playing Ted Bundy, and when he looks so *ordinary*, we think he is ordinary.

Normally, there's no way to collect on these

guys because they're long gone by the time you discover what they're up to. The only way to deal with this kind of individual is to stay out of their path. *See "How Can You Identify a Scoundrel?" in "Pre-Business Check."*

WHERE TO START

Before you sue, consider this... Is he the sort of scoundrel who would consider a legal judgment as a moral obligation to pay?

To assess your scoundrel's worth (or worthlessness) check with...

THE RECORDER'S OFFICE: Look for abstract judgments and mechanic's liens where your scoundrel is the grantee. This means that he has lost a suit in court and has not paid. Not a pretty sight.

SUPERIOR & MUNICIPAL CLERK'S OFFICE: If there are a lot of cases listed against your pal, then he could be a professional scoundrel. Request the file, and you'll find out everything you ever wanted to know. And then some.

DOES HE HAVE THE MONEY?

If the above tests have dampened your spirits regarding your pursuit to sue, relax. So far, we've just been assessing what kind of a character you're up against.

The true test is...Does he have the money? You don't have to find it yet, you just have to know that there is, indeed, a pot at the end of the rainbow.

The type of assets you'll look for will depend upon the size of your claim. If he owes you $200, a steady job as a mechanic's assistant will do just fine. If he owes you a million bucks, then he better own the shop. And a few more like it.

Check out the following...

HOUSE AND CAR: What kind of a house does he live in? What kind of a car does he drive? I once had a man try to hire me to collect from a 70 year-old man who lived in a government subsidized retirement home and rode the streetcar. I turned down a shot at a possible $37,000 commission because I just didn't believe the guy had the money.

RECORDER'S OFFICE: As long as you're there...look through the Grantor/Grantee index for at least five years. Does he own property? Does he regularly buy and sell property? Or is he about to get booted out of his abode via a trustee's sale? What does he owe on his mortgage? Get snoopy! All these things are good indications of financial stability or instability.

COUNTY CLERK'S OFFICE: Is there a divorce record? Check all the way back to infinity. These are the most helpful of any records that you will find anywhere. If your scoundrel was divorced recently and there was no property or possessions to divide, then the news is not good. If anybody knows how much money a guy has, it's his ex-wife.

MUNICIPAL COUNTY CLERK: Check out all cases, but pay particular attention to unlawful detainers. My theory is, if a guy is running out of money, the last thing he quits paying is his rent. (Unless he's that rare breed of scoundrel who gets a big kick out of lifting heavy boxes.)

By now you should have a pretty good idea of your scoundrel's net worth. Again, consider it in relation to the size of your claim. If he's a millionaire, and all you need is $200, then it may be more difficult to attach his Porsche than it would be to garnish the wages of a working man.

POP QUIZ

Now that you've read this chapter, take this quiz. Answer the questions truthfully. Remember, if you lie to yourself, or copy the answers from your neighbor, you'll just be hurting yourself.

TRUE OR FALSE

1. My scoundrel voluntarily pays his bills as evidenced by the lack of judgments against him in the county courthouse.

2. My scoundrel has a job.

3. He or she has been working steadily, as in career-type, and is not likely to bolt should he or she receive an attachment of wages.

4. If my scoundrel does not have a job, he or she has some other means of support other than income from welfare, social security, unem-

ployment, disability or a pension.

5.   Said scoundrel has a bank account, and I know where it is.

6.   Said scoundrel possesses real property, other than the place of residence.

7.   If a business is involved, it is solvent and has a good reputation for paying its bills.

SCORE

TRUE: 6-7 You don't have a care in the world. In fact, I'm surprised you bought this book to begin with.

TRUE: 4-5 Your chances of collecting are pretty good. All your scoundrel needs is a little shove. Tread lightly, it might be easier to work with the alleged jerk and set up a payment plan, than to sue prematurely.

TRUE: 1-3 You have a long road to travel, but you ought to be able to collect at least part of your money. Become the kind of person your scoundrel won't want in his life.

TRUE: 0 Smear peanut butter all over this book and then try to return it to your local bookstore. You'll have about as much chance of getting your money back as you have of collecting from your scoundrel.

The Clues

"You can't find a rich guy in the Motel 6 Lounge."
Rat Dog Dick Company Motto

Knowledge is power. You probably already know more about your scoundrel than you ever wanted to know.

For example.... Whenever I go searching for a scoundrel, the most valuable thing I ever hope to find is a divorce record. That's because the ex-wife knows more about, and tells more about, my subject than anyone else on earth. Yet, ironically, these are the same women who end up hiring me to collect their child support. They have a wealth of information at their disposal, but because they don't know where he keeps the dough, they think what they do know is insignificant.

Not so! Everything you know about someone is important. Not so much because of what you know, but because it will lead you to things you don't know.

For example, take the date of birth. Now the date of birth may not seem important to you now, since you've probably already crossed this guy off your present-giving list. So why would you want to know when his birthday is? In case you want to figure out his astrological rising?

No, silly. Because, in some states, if you know his date of birth you can run a driver's license check at the Department of Motor Vehicles and find an address. A handy thing to know, if you're after his loot.

And where do you find his date of birth, if you were never on party list terms with the birthday boy to begin with?

Plenty of places. Traffic court in the county where he lived, for one. Voter's registration in that county. His marriage license listed with the county, or the Department of Vital Statistics at the state level.

So you see. If he ever voted, or got married, or got a traffic ticket, it means he can never really drop out of sight again. Get the picture?

WHERE DO I GO, WHAT DO I DO?

To the county courthouse. That's where you'll find the clues.

At the county seat of every county there stands a block or more of government buildings. In these buildings you will find all the records from all the dealings in that county gathered together and indexed alphabetically.

Here's a rundown of the County Offices. Just as you may live in a parish rather than a county, the

24

names of these offices may be different. For example, what is called the Secretary of State in California is referred to as the Corporation Commission in Arizona. I used the California names because those are the ones I know best, and because, let's face it, I had to call them something.

THE ASSESSOR'S OFFICE   Ownership of Real Property.

*   Property listed by Owner's name
*   Property listed by Address (Situs)
*   Property listed by Parcel number

THE RECORDERS OFFICE   Liens against Real Property

*   GRANTEE\GRANTOR INDEX
  Listing of all property transferred or sold
  Tax liens
  Judgments
  Abstract judgments
  Notices and defaults

*   STATE INDEX OF VITAL STATISTICS
  All marriages in the state over a span of years
  All births in the state for a span of years
  All deaths for same

*   COUNTY INDEX OF VITAL STATISTICS
  A listing, and the corresponding documentation of all marriages, deaths and births recorded in that county since the beginning of time to present.

VOTER'S REGISTRATION

* <u>VOTERS INDEX</u>: A listing of all registered voters in that county, indexed by subject's name.

* <u>SITUS INDEX:</u> A listing of registered voters, indexed by address.

SUPERIOR COUNTY CLERK

* <u>PLAINTIFFS & DEFENDANTS INDEX:</u> A listing of all civil suits initiated in that county. Sometimes Plaintiffs and Defendants are listed in one index and sometimes separately.

* <u>FICTITIOUS BUSINESS NAME INDEX:</u> A listing of all businesses registered in the county. Usually indexed by owner's name, and by the name of the business.

* <u>PROBATE INDEX:</u> Index of all cases involving the dispensation of an individual's property upon his death. Listed by the name of the deceased.

* <u>CRIMINAL INDEX:</u> Listing of all criminal action against an individual, by subject's name.

MUNICIPAL COUNTY CLERK

* <u>CIVIL INDEX:</u> Plaintiff's and Defendant's index for cases tried at the Municipal Court level.

* <u>SMALL CLAIMS INDEX:</u> Can be with the Civil Index, or listed separately.

*   CRIMINAL INDEX: Evictions. Drunk driving. Bad Checks.

*   TRAFFIC INDEX: Listing of all traffic infractions, by subject's name.

TAX COLLECTOR'S OFFICE

*   SECURED TAX ROLLS: A list of taxable real property. Similar or identical to the property owner's index in the Assessor's Office.

*   UNSECURED TAX ROLLS: A list of businesses which pay taxes.

*   FISHING & HUNTING LICENSES: By name.

*   PET LICENSES: By owner's name, not by Rover's.

BUILDING DEPARTMENT

*   Files for improvements on real property located in unincorporated parts of the county. Usually listed by address.

PLANNING DEPARTMENT

*   Files for zoning variances, etc., in unincorporated parts of the county. Listed by name, address, or assessor's parcel number.

LIBRARY

*   Newspaper morgue

* Reverse directories
* Almost everything else ever printed

DEPARTMENT OF MOTOR VEHICLES

* DRIVERS LICENSE INFORMATION: Usually accessible by full name, date of birth or driver's license number.

* VEHICLE INFORMATION: Ownership accessible by plate number.

* ALPHA SEARCH: Generic computer search by name and area. It will reveal ownership of vehicles, boats, and sometimes airplanes and the address of the owner.

CITY OFFICES

* BUSINESS LICENSES

* BUILDING PERMITS for property within the city

POST OFFICE

* Forwarding addresses

DEPARTMENT OF CONSUMER AFFAIRS

* Businesses and professions regulated by the state.

SECRETARY OF STATE:
CORPORATE STATUS DIVISION

* Corporations and their officers. Listed by name of the corporation. In some states, also by owner's name.

ALCOHOL CONTROL BOARD

* Index of liquor licenses by bar name, or owner's name.

NATIONAL DRIVER REGISTER SERVICE

* A national index of suspended or revoked licenses.

MILITARY RECORDS

* Air Force
* Army
* Navy
* Coast Guard

CREDIT REPORTING AGENCIES

* TRW
* CBI

SOCIAL SECURITY

* Will give out no information, and forward mail only.

These are the places that hold the clues to the identity, location and assets of your scoundrel. In the chapter entitled, *"Where to Find the Dough,"* there will be more specific information on what you will find in these offices, as well as why you want to know this information.

4

How To Collect Without Going To Court

"Why spend dollars on costly overhead when you can hire someone who works out of a phone booth at Hunt's Donuts?"

A Satisfied Customer

The major part of this book deals with how to collect on a bad debt after a legal judgment is in place. That is because you cannot legally separate a man from his money until the court says you can.

There are, however, some things you can do before you actually sue. Remember, these are intimidation measures only and any scoundrel worth his salt will know that. Hopefully, though, you might have stumbled upon a stupid or novice scoundrel.

31

A GENTLEMAN AND A SCOUNDREL

I once did a very naughty thing. I assumed that the attorney who hired me was not a scoundrel.

Richard Hendrex was a hot shot lawyer in San Francisco. He was a fortyish, silver-haired, silver-tongued, baby-blue-eyed charmer. He had a nice smile and a big office in a renovated Victorian with a lot of other hot shot lawyers. Altogether, a good date.

One day his secretary called in a panic. Hendrex needed some information and he had to have it that day. It involved only a few hours work, but he was desperate.

Her boss, Richard Hendrex was representing a tenant whose landlord was trying to evict him in order to raise the rent on his rent-controlled apartment. The scam was that he, the landlord, needed to move into the apartment because he was getting a divorce. This method is one of the only ways a San Francisco landlord can evict someone who is regularly paying their rent.

The case was simple enough. A trip to the San Mateo County Courthouse revealed that yes, he had filed divorce proceedings several months before, but there was no action since, and no attorney was involved in the original action. The alleged divorce looked like a red herring.

Also, the landlord and his wife owned a half-million dollar mansion in Atherton. Divorce or no divorce, would he really want to move into a tenement slum in the Mission District when he owned a half dozen other properties?

I took a drive over to the mansion where his wife cheerfully assured me that he would be "home" soon.

Case solved. Everybody was happy except the landlord.

And Rat Dog.

Enter Scoundrel Number Two: Richard Hendrex.

I billed him and requested my usual payment in thirty days. When he neglected to send me my hundred dollar check for two and a half months I was not overly concerned. So far he wasn't doing anything different than most of the attorneys I worked for. When I went to his office, he apologized, hustled me away from the clients and slipped me a check.

Which bounced.

He gave me another check. It bounced.

I went for triple damages, which is the law in California, and won the suit. Now Hendrex owed me three hundred dollars. And he still wasn't paying.

Embarrassing! The future author of *A Private Eye's Guide to Collecting a Bad Debt* suckered by a scoundrel!

It was then that I hit upon a solution which could have produced results even without going to court (although I would not have collected triple damages.)

I called the California Bar Association. They sympathized but said they had no authority over an attorney and his victims, only over an attorney and his clients. I told them to send me a complaint form anyway. I filled it out, xeroxed it and then mailed a copy to Richard Hendrex.

Suddenly the check was in the mail. Unlike his other checks, it cleared.

Apparently Hendrex didn't want the Bar Association to know what everybody else already knew. He was a scoundrel!

As a postscript to this story...

Years later, I ran into Hendrex's secretary at a

party in Marin.

She had gotten a big kick out of my collection practices, as I was one of the few who had gotten money out of her boss. She had, in fact, been his girlfriend during the time I had been taken and he still owed her a couple of thousand bucks. (For being his secretary, not for being his girlfriend.) He had also stretched out his office rent for as long as was legally possible. He had filed writs and amendments and whatever else there exists for as long as he could. He did not, in fact, leave until the sheriff came and took him away.

As of this writing, Richard Hendrex is no longer in private practice in San Francisco. He now works for the public defender's office!

PREVENTING PROBLEMS

The best way to clear up your collection problems is, obviously, not to get in trouble in the first place. (Here comes the "I told you so" part.) If you are in business, analyze what it is that is causing the problem.

I once had a client who wanted me to help him collect on a series of worthless out of state checks. He sold merchandise by mail order and accepted c.o.d.'s as payment. The problem came when the recipient gave him a bad check to pay for the merchandise. He was stuck with dozens of bad checks and no way to inexpensively sue these out of state deadbeats.

There was nothing I could do to help him. I explained that the reason he was getting bad checks was because the people ordering the merchandise were scoundrels! They knew he couldn't effectively collect across state lines, and that's why they ordered from him instead of from a local source. He was playing right into their hands!

My client had no choice but to write off these debts. However, he did change his business practices. Instead of accepting personal checks, he accepted only money orders for c.o.d. orders. By changing his business practices, he eliminated an entire source of stress from his life.

GOOD BUSINESS PRACTICES

No book on debt-collecting, not even the best book ever written by anyone, anywhere in the world, can replace not having to buy a book at all.

Take it from me, if you let your clientele know, right away, that you expect to be paid and paid on time, you'll save yourself a lot of grief.

I know, whereof I speak.

You see, I used to run the Rat Dog Dick Detective Agency in quite a slipshod manner. I'd finish a case, call up the client with the outcome and the amount of the bill, and then file the scribblings on the far corner of my desk, confident that a check would be forthcoming.

When the check didn't come, and it never did, I barely noticed. I knew I was broke, and I knew I had a very messy desk, but I just never put the two together.

Then came panicsville. The rent was due and I was busted! In desperation, I did the same thing I always do whenever I'm broke. I indulged in a mega case of combined avoidance behavior and desk cleaning. In the process, of course, I'd find a lot of old invoices that had never been paid. I'd then pull all these scribblings together, recreate a bill, and send it out, again expecting immediate results.

The crisis would pass, as crises tend to do, and then I'd remember I *still* hadn't been paid. I'd call back the client and ask, "Hey, did you ever get that invoice I sent you? No? Oh well, I'll send you another." Six weeks later I'd call again. "Oh great, you got it! When do you think you can pay it?"

Needless to say, I was a very poor person.

The upshot of all this is, if a client doesn't get a bill for three months, they think they have three months more to pay. In other words, if it's not important to you, why should it be important to them? And if it takes you six months to get past the point of asking nicely, then you may be unconsciously contributing to the delinquency of a scoundrel.

Think of it like this. The statute of limitations on most bills is three or four years, depending upon the state and the type of debt. If you only make a phone call every four months, all your scoundrel has to do is avoid your babbling nine times and he's home free!

Here are some ground rules to incorporate in your accounts/receivable program. (See Appendix A)

1. All one-time retail customers must pay in advance or c.o.d.. No exceptions! ("Sorry, company policy.") This goes double for out-of-state, as these debts are doubly difficult to collect on. If a customer balks, be gentle. He's probably just upset that he's not going to be able to bilk you.

2. Do not give credit until a customer qualifies, either through credit checks or by using your services for a period of six months to a year.

3.   Check out credit references. *Soooo* many times a client will hand me an application they took from a scoundrel and the whole thing will be lies. Don't be afraid to *not* trust strangers.

4.   Set up a billing schedule. Send it immediately upon delivery of the goods or services. Terms are 30 days, no longer.

5.   If you have not received payment in 30 days, send a second notice. Stamp "30 DAY NOTICE" all over it. Charge 1% interest on the unpaid balance. Do not ship any more merchandise until you receive payment.

6.   Send a third notice at 60 days. Add on the interest. Follow it up with a phone call.

7.   In 90 days, send a fourth notice, marked "FINAL NOTICE" and send it registered mail. Be sure and add the interest. Include a letter stating that if you do not receive payment in 15 days you will begin legal proceedings. Advise that the scoundrel will be libel not only for the invoice and interest, but for legal costs, process serving fees and other expenses incurred in the collection process. Enclose a photocopy of the original invoice and any signed contracts.

8.   Fifteen days later, do it! Do not threaten to sue unless you intend to do it. The last thing you need is for your scoundrel to lose respect for you. And many times a scoundrel will not act until he has a subpoena in hand.

ALTERNATIVES TO SUING

There are, of course, alternatives to suing.

If you are dealing with a client whose intentions are honorable, he's just in a cash-flow crunch, you will want to preserve the relationship. If so, consider these alternatives.

BAD CHECKS

If your scoundrel has passed a bad check, it might not be as worthless as you think. Every day, call the bank. Give them the account number, his name, and the amount of the check. Ask the clerk if there are sufficient funds to cover the amount. This is common practice, and if the bank knows your scoundrel they're waiting for your call. Call often, but especially around the first of the month when people tend to stock pile their money in order to pay the rent. When the funds show up, stop everything and...go get the money!

PAYMENT PLAN

Don't sue prematurely. If your scoundrel is willing to pay his debt to you through any kind of a reasonable schedule, take it. Collecting on a judgment is a very difficult process and sometimes the best you can do is to get partial payment of the judgment. As long as you are receiving some money, you're better off than trying to find and attach his wages later.

BARTER SYSTEM

Offer to let your scoundrel settle his debt by providing you with goods or services instead of money. Get a lifetime supply of carpet cleaning, or maybe that nice BMW motorcycle in his driveway.

COMPLAINT DEPARTMENT

Another trick, pre or post judgment, is to go the complaint department route. If your scoundrel is a businessman or in any of the professions governed by city, state or federal government, you have his nose hairs in a vice.

First, obtain a complaint form from the agency which governs that profession. Then fill it out and send it back, along with a duplicate copy to the scoundrel. Even if the agency will not settle disputes between a businessman and his suppliers, the scoundrel might not know that. Even smart scoundrels like Richard Hendrex don't like to call their governing agency and say, "Uh...can you tell me...would it tick you guys off a lot if I stopped paying all my bills?"

THE "FLATTERY WILL GET YOU A FREEBIE" SCAM

Trust your instincts. If something looks fishy, check it out. It's better to keep your money in the first place, than have to try and get it back later.

When this book was first published, a columnist from the San Francisco Examiner covered it for the newspaper. The morning after the article was printed I received a phone call from a John Howie of

"West Coast Review" requesting a copy of my book for review. He gave me a post office box number in San Francisco and hung up.

I was elated! I was going to be reviewed by West Coast Review, whatever that was. I packed the book up and put the postage on it. Then I got kind of curious. What was West Coast Review, anyway? Is there such a thing as freelance reviewers who write book reviews and then attempts to sell them to periodicals? Could I expect to end up in the Wall Street Journal or the New York Times?

I decided to call back John Howie and ask, so I looked up the West Coast Review in a directory that lists media markets.

Not there.

I checked the city telephone directory.

Nope. Not there, either.

In desperation, I flipped to the "H's" and perused the Howies. No John.

By now I was suspicious. So I called and asked which post office housed the box number that John Howie gave me. Then I drove the book down there in person.

Now, postal clerks are very closed mouthed about releasing the identity of box holders if it is a privately held box. However, if a box is registered in a company name and you have ordered but not received merchandise from that company, then the clerk should supply you with the name and actual street address of the business.

When I asked if the box was registered to "West Coast Review" she confirmed what I already suspected. The box was leased to a private individual. And that person's name was not John Howie.

I thanked the clerk, picked up the book and left. Needless to say, I never got reviewed by "West Coast Review."

But then "John Howie" never got a free copy of my book either!

DON'T GET TOO PARANOID

Not everyone is a scoundrel. Sure, check people out before you do business with them, but don't get too cynical.

As a postscript to the above story...

About a year after I thwarted the alleged John Howie's futile attempt to get a free copy of my book, I went to the American Booksellers Association trade show in Washington D.C. There, outside, each morning was a man handing out sample copies of a magazine called "West Coast Review."

Boy, what some people won't do to get a free copy of my book!

THE "MY BROTHER BET ME YOU WOULDN'T MARRY ME" SCAM

Another way to avoid problems is to not marry people you have just met. Especially if you happened to mention on your first date that your spouse just died and left you a wealthy widow.

Okay, I'm sorry, I know this seems obvious but trust me, people are still doing it.

Maria Goodman came to me with a very interesting story. I found it interesting, Maria found it suicidal.

Maria was almost sixty but was still an attractive woman. Her hair was black, Clairol #29, her skin clear and her eyes bright. She had worked for almost twenty years at a famous watering hole, a favorite of tourists, on the edge of the seedy Tenderloin section in San Francisco.

One day a man about her age came in. He returned the next day. And the next. Soon he was a regular.

Every day when Wilfred paid his bill, they talked a little more. He told Maria he was from a little town in Texas and had been widowed for fifteen years. He imported cars from Germany, one by one, to fill special orders. He had business dealings in Texas, New York, and Philadelphia.

They dated for about three weeks, and then he said he had to go out of town on business. He'd be gone about a month. Ten days later Wilfred called and asked her to pick him up from the airport. When she did, he had all his things with him. He went home with her that night and never left.

At first Wilfred took her out to dinner quite a lot. They talked of their past lives, the $100 thousand Certificate of Deposit her husband had left her, and Wilfred's own vast financial holdings.

Soon, wealthy though he was, he had a cash flow problem. (Hey, these things happen!) She started picking up the tabs. He started ordering lobster.

One day he told her he knew how they could make a great windfall. It seems he had told his brother all about her and his brother bet him "a lot of money" that she wouldn't marry him. If only she would, he said, gazing into her eyes, he'd win the bet and they'd be rich, rich, rich!

Oh Wilfred, you silver-tongued devil!

Maria did marry him, but she never saw the proceeds from the bet. As it turned out there were a lot of things she never saw, or never saw again. And it was only a matter of time until Wilfred was one of them.

By the time she hired me, Maria had been with Wilfred for two years and without him for two weeks. And he wasn't much on goodbyes or letter writing, if you get my drift.

I was a little confused as to why Maria Goodman hired me. Did she want me to find him? Did she want him back? Had he taken any money from her? And did she want it back?

No, she said. None of the above. She just wanted to know the truth. It seemed she didn't know much about old Wilfred, and what she did know didn't make much sense.

In the two years that Maria and Wilfred were an item, it seems he had never once made a telephone call from the house. He always used his telex number, and she'd never even seen any of the bills. In fact, there was not anywhere, one scrap of paper with a name or telephone number or anything pertaining to him or his business.

Whenever her husband referred to anyone it was by either their first or last name. His attorney was "Rudding." However there was no attorney named Rudding listed with the California Bar Association who admitted to having Wilfred for a client.

I never found out anything about Wilfred except that he was a liar.

On their marriage certificate he had listed "retired farmer" as his profession. Yet he told Maria he was a car importer. His birth date was listed on the certificate as a few days different than what she remembered he had told her. He said his first wife had been dead for fifteen years, and yet the certificate stated he had been widowed for twenty.

Wilfred told Maria he had bought her a home in Santa Rosa from a man named Gobbly. He also said that a neighbor named Jordon was looking after the yard. She couldn't see the house because it wasn't yet "perfect."

I checked with the Sonoma County Assessor's Office, but there was no house in Santa Rosa listed in her or her husband's name. There was no man named Gobbly who, in the last year, had sold property in that county. Per the telephone directory, there was only one "Gobbly" listed, and checking the Assessor's records and the Haines Reverse Directory, he did not live next door to a Mr. Jordon.

There was no death certificate for her husband's late wife in all of Texas. There was no driver's license listed for him in California or Texas. There was no car dealer named Goodman listed with the German automobile manufacturer, nor with the city of San Francisco.

Maria Goodman's husband never returned. Her CD is, at this writing, still intact, and she has stern instructions from me not to take out any life insurance policies on herself or to change her will.

Luckily, I never found other marriages for Wilfred Goodman over the years in the state of California. Either that was not his name at all, or Maria was his only victim in that state.

We never found out the truth about her husband, his true name, where he was from, or why he lied about the house.

What we did know was that for his own reasons he chose to marry her, misrepresent himself, live off her salary for a year and then disappear.

Personally, I think Maria Goodman got off lucky.

COLLECTION TECHNIQUES
THAT YOU CAN USE

Most techniques used by collection agencies are things you can do yourself. In fact, because collection agencies are very strictly governed, and because they can lose their licenses if they goof up, you actually have a bit more leeway. After all, the state can't take away your license, unless you have one. You should, however, stay within the legal limits of harassment. I mean after all, fair is fair.

Your initial letters should suggest politely that the scoundrel (I wouldn't call him that, some of them can get quite cranky) has overlooked his last payment. You, the creditor, would appreciate his payment at the earliest convenience (which better be soon). Subsequent correspondence should become more and more assertive, stopping just short of threats to property, his family and his personal body. Be sure to mention your attorney a lot. (See letters in Appendix A)

Here are some points to make in your correspondence...

1.   Get the debtor to admit the debt, and agree to pay. Get it in writing.

2.   Let him know that you can and will sue. Make a point of mentioning any assets of his that he knows that you know he has. Save the ones that he doesn't know that you know he has to use as your trump card.

3.   Let him know that you are not above contacting

45

a credit reporting agency, such as TRW or CBI about his debt.

4.   Never make an accusation of fraud or criminal activity. It never hurts, however, to throw in a little zinger like "merchandise obtained under false pretenses, or credit obtained through false statements are both acts of fraud."

5.   Send a "pre-summons notice." This is drawn up to resemble a court order, complete with notary stamp. It lists the amount of debt, and the appropriate court action including costs and legal fees. It also states a deadline for the payment of the debt.

6.   Ask for a small amount of money as a "gesture of goodwill." Payment of any kind is considered an acknowledgement of debt by the court. It also reactivates the statue of limitations and keeps the debt alive.

7.   If you have received a bad check, remind him that passing a bad check can result in a jail sentence.

8.   Also remind him of your right to collect triple damages on a bad check, if this is your state's policy.

POPULAR EXCUSES AMONG SCOUNDRELS TO AVOID PAYMENT

A common practice among scoundrels is to stall until you either give up or until the statute of limitations runs out. These are the most common excuses known to scoundrels...

1.   The merchandise is not satisfactory. He keeps asking for adjustments on the bill.

2.   The bill has already been paid. He writes you often and with vehemence.

3.   He stalls, claiming that he isn't working, has other debts or expenses, or that he is sick. He swears his good faith and honest intentions, but sends no money. He is not specific about when he will.

LAST CHANCE: THE COLLECTION AGENCIES.

Collection agencies are private companies that specialize in collecting debts. I see no reason to hire one unless you are too timid to be threatening or too busy to do the work yourself.

Collection agencies work on a percentage of the money that is collected. It is usually about 30% to 50% of the gross, depending upon how difficult they think it will be to collect.

It is also a common practice to accept cash settlements far below the amount of the debt. This eliminates months of frustrating work that they would spend in trying to collect the whole amount. Unscrupulous companies may never even inform you of a settlement, and so you will receive nothing.

In 1989, 6,000 U.S. collection agencies handled accounts totalling over 72 *billion* dollars. They recovered about 18%, and after deducting an average fee of 34%, passed along $8.8 billion to their clients.

What's the bottom line? Give a collection agency an account of $1 to collect, and expect to see about $.12 of it!

STATUTE OF LIMITATIONS FOR CIVIL ACTIONS

Don't waste too much time trying to suck money back out of a leech. There is a time limit on initiating the collection of a bill. This is figured from the date of the last payment. So if you can get even ten bucks out of the slime, it will keep the debt alive.

Suing The So & So

"I never carry a gun. I never lie to anyone's mother. And I only repossess cars from members of my immediate family."

Rat Dog Dick

So you've decided to sue. Good for you! Don't let the bum get away with it.

The hardest thing about suing can be getting the sucker served. True scoundrels spend their lives denying who they are, and where they live. I swear, it takes more energy than just paying up!

49

FREDERICKS OF SCOUNDRELWOOD

Melanie Connolly was just such a scoundrel. She'd changed her name so many times that even she'd gotten confused.

Melanie had bought a car from Sweet Walter Black. She'd made a couple of payments and then crashed and burned the thing. Naturally she didn't want to go on paying Sweet Walter. She was sure that Sweet Walter would understand. Well, he didn't. So he hired me to find and serve a summons on Melanie.

There was no information on Melanie Connolly in the County Courthouse, but there was a traffic ticket for Melanie Connolly-Freestone. Switching my search to Melanie Freestone, I found a lady with quite a sordid past. Addresses popped up. Other names. Eviction notices. Small claims suits. Judgments everywhere. This lady could have been an entire career for a budding Melvin Belli.

Address Number One: Gone. Only a three day notice from the phone company marked her passing.

Address Number Two: Closer. A white haired grandma said, yes, she'd rented a room to Melanie, but she didn't come around much anymore. She had, although, left some of her things. Would I care to snoop through them? (Being a P.I. of high character, I did not, of course. But I couldn't help noticing somewhere near the top of one pile some samples from a nationally known lingerie company.)

Address Number Three: The condo of an old boyfriend - an address that Melanie had given Sweet Walter long ago, and then later told him she'd moved. When Sweet Walter phoned there, the boyfriend called her some nasty names and confirmed the split.

I arrived just as a real estate agent was showing the place. She said it was owned by Bob and Melanie

Something, and that Melanie Something would be home about six. And so I positioned myself outside with a National Enquirer (having an inquiring mind and all) and a cup of coffee. When the coffee and the Enquirer were finished, I went on to speculating why city officials never put public restrooms in residential districts.

Pretty soon a lady fitting Melanie's description drove up and went into the condo. In her car were lingerie samples. The license plate matched.

I rang the buzzer. I banged on the door. I yelled up at the open window. I did it all again. Pretty soon the lady answered.

"Melanie Connolly-Freestone Something?" I asked.

"Sorry," she said, shutting the door.

"Oh no you don't, Melanie," I countered, blocking the door with my foot. "You look like Melanie Connolly, you drive her car and you live with her boyfriend. Now, if you're not Melanie Connolly, then she's gonna want to know who you are!" I shoved the summons between her knees. I guess I should have left, but all that coffee was making me irritable.

"And another thing, Melanie," I said. "You ought to be ashamed of yourself! Do you have any idea how much you've upset Sweet Walter Black, not to mention about half of the people in Marin? You're ruining people's entire days! Get a life!"

"I'm not Melanie Connolly," the lady said evenly.

"Tell it to the judge!" I hissed and slammed her door in her face.

The really ironic part is that she'd half convinced me she wasn't Melanie Connolly. What if I'd bawled out some unsuspecting underwear saleslady? It wasn't until Melanie called Sweet Walter and set up a payment plan that I felt better.

51

SINGING SUBPOENAS

Just as there is such a thing as judgment-proof, there is also such a thing as subpoena-proof. Or, at least, there used to be.

I once had to serve a man who lived in an expensive condo complex down by the waterfront in San Francisco. Because I didn't know where he worked I had to serve him at home. It was a high security building and I knew better than to even try to talk my way past the security guard downstairs. To make matters even more difficult, I didn't know what he looked like, so I couldn't catch him coming out of the building. His car was locked up in the under-ground garage, so I'd never be able to identify him by catching him getting into his car. In order to serve the guy, I had to get into the building.

That's when I came up with the idea of "Singing Subpoenas."

As luck would have it, I was taking tap dancing classes at the time, so I had this really terrific costume that I hadn't even had a chance to wear yet. Bright blue with pink sequins and a blue fringe skirt. It even had a big pink feather to wear in your hair. Real Rockette stuff.

Thusly attired, I easily talked my way in past the security guard. I mean who's going to refuse entry to a singing telegram person in a really great looking costume? And, as an extra plus, the guard couldn't even call ahead to announce me. I mean these things are supposed to be a surprise!

And, believe me, it was. When the guy opened the door I belted out a couple of choruses of "You made me sue you! I didn't want to do it!" laid paper on him and split before he even figured out that he shouldn't be smiling.

LEGAL HELP

Most cities have a legal service which will rec-
ommend a qualified attorney who may offer you a free
hour of consultation. Look under "Attorneys" in the
Yellow Pages for "Attorney Referral Service."

Also, there is of late, a fairly new concept in the
law profession known as "legal insurance." For a fee,
you can join a service and have, among other features,
unlimited access to an 800 number offering "pre-paid"
legal advice. These companies will give you an idea of
the validity of your claim and your chances of winning
in court. Depending upon the fees and coverage, they
may even represent you in court. Some unions and
credit unions have similar plans. In any case, look in
the directory under Legal Services, or ask your local
bar association for a list of pre-paid legal service
companies operating in your area.

THE COURTS

Your case will be heard in either Small Claims
Court, Municipal Court or Superior Court, depending
upon the type of action and the dollar amount of the
claim. If your case falls under the jurisdiction of
Municipal or Superior Court, you have little choice but
to hire an attorney. If, however, your suit is eligible for
Small Claims Court, neither side is allowed, by law, to
be represented by an attorney.

Here is what you can expect....

1. Go to the Small Claims Division of the county
    courthouse where the claim originated or where
    the defendant (aka scoundrel) lives. Fill out a
    one-pager stating your claim. Be sure and bring

all the pertinent information such as dates, correct spelling of the name, and the address of the defendant. It is important that you list all parties concerned, as you can collect from any one of them.

2. The clerk will give you a court date. Try to get one that will conflict with your scoundrel's schedule. This is done for spite. It will also mean that your scoundrel will be less likely to show up in court and you will win by default. Unfortunately, it also means, the court is more likely to overturn the judgment, should the defendant request it. But then, them's the breaks.

3. Serve the summons.

REGISTERED OR CERTIFIED MAIL The clerk can usually send it for you. But if the defendant does not sign for it personally, it is not considered properly served, and it will have to be served again.

PROCESS SERVER Along with the cost, ask the process server how many attempts they will make before they call it quits. Try to find one who will keep trying until the deed is done.

HIRE A FRIEND If you are really cheap, or think you might lose in court (and therefore have to pay the service fee yourself) you can get a friend to serve the summons. Anyone who is over 18 years old and not a party to the action can do it. However, the laws are so strict on service, and the consequences so devastating if it is not done properly, that I suggest you hire a pro.

SERVICE BY PUBLICATION. In extreme cases where the defendant cannot be located, he can be served by placing a notice in the newspaper. This is known as last chance service.

4. Show up in court. Bring any contracts, work-sheets, or other documents to back up your claim. You may even bring a witness. If your scoundrel doesn't show up...congratulations! Unless your claim is really off the wall, you've won by default.

    If he does show, you must tell your story to the court. Stick to the point and don't lose your temper. Usually the judge will mail you the results in a few days. Expect to win, lose or draw.

5. Wait for the check. Even if you know it's not coming, wait at least thirty days. Check with the court to see what the time limit is for your scoundrel to appeal the court's decision.

6. After the time for appeal lapses, write him a friendly note reminding him of the debt and the court's decision.

7. When he ignores your letter (and he will), pro-ceed to the next chapter. Take every penny the scum has and leave him to die alone in a gutter.

VACATING THE JUDGMENT

The three dirtiest words in the collection business. Vacating the judgment means the court has set aside the judgment and the case has to be retried. This normally happens in an uncontested case when the scoundrel finds out that you can, in fact, take his money away from him. He will be quite unconcerned all the while you are suing him, never raise an eyebrow when you win, and then scream like the dickens when you start collecting. Trouble is, judges fall for this.

One of the primary reasons judgments are set aside is because the defendant claims he was improperly served. One way to safeguard against this is to make sure the defendant is served *personally* instead of being *subserved.* If he is personally served, he cannot claim he was unaware of the suit. He must, instead, come up with a good reason why he didn't defend himself in court. There are time stipulations as well. If the summons was served even one day late, there is a good chance the judgment can be vacated.

A REAL LIFE, VERY SAD STORY

Once upon a time, in the state of California, I served a woman who lived 30 miles from my home. My client went to court, won the suit and then, while entering the judgment, the clerk discovered that I had left out one letter when I filled out the proof of service. The clerk threw the entire judgment out of court. Because of this, the summons had to be re-served (for which, of course I was not paid) and the entire case retried before my client could even attempt collection.

This is why I strongly suggest hiring a professional. And not me!

Skiptracing

"*Do I know Rat Dog? I spit on her grave! I finally lost her somewhere between the Place de la Concorde and the northbound entrance to the Golden Gate Bridge!*"

Maddie Bunshee,
Scoundrel

Skiptracing is simply the process of finding a missing person. This is not to say that this person even knows that he is missing. Chances are he knows right where he is. He's hiding from you!

There are many books written on skiptracing, and I've read every one I've found. But it is not my intention to write a book within a book. I will, therefore, give you the abridged edition of the skip-tracer's guide to locating a scoundrel. With it, even the nastiest of the breed can usually be located in a minimum of steps. This means that instead of sorting through ten years of leads, you can know where he was a year ago and go from there. You might even get lucky and put your finger right on the little bugger.

The basic rule of skiptracing is to follow every lead to its end. Then follow those leads to their ends. Do this until you find the person, or die of old age.

Here goes...

1. The obvious. Call the operator. (This information is up-to-the-minute, unlike the phone book.) If he/she is not listed in your area, call the operators in all the surrounding areas and neighboring counties. Also, call any counties where he or she might own property. Your friend might not be a scoundrel at all. Maybe he just got a great deal on a condo in Petaluma.

2. Go to the County Courthouse. (See *Where to Find the Dough*) Then check out the indexes in the Municipal Court, Traffic Court, Superior Court, Assessor's Office, Recorder's Office, Voter's Registration, and Criminal Court. Note any addresses. Don't eliminate a source just because a processes server stated that the defendant was no longer on the premises. Scoundrels have been known to lie about their identity.

Pay particular attention to these sources: Voter's Registration, Marriage Licenses, Traffic Tickets, Birth Certificates.

All of them contain the most devastating information known to scoundrels: the dreaded *date of birth!*

3.   Go to the Assessor's Office. Check out all the addresses that you have found. Do they belong to:

THE SCOUNDREL

a.   This means he is likely to answer the door himself and (if you have never met him) lie about his identity.

b.   The property is rented. This means that, most likely, the tenant knows the whereabouts of his landlord. (It also means that you can attach the income from this property when you are ready to collect.)

A RELATIVE OF THE SCOUNDREL   Could be friend or foe, good guy or liar. To determine the credibility of the source, you need as much information as possible before you knock.

SOMEONE UNRELATED, BUT WHO LIVES THERE   You can deduce this by putting together several sources of information. Do the tax bills go to the address of the property? If so, the person owning the house also lives there. Is there a homeowner's exemption? (A tax credit a property owner can claim on his primary place of residence.) Again, you can deduce that the owner of the property lives there.

Now, who is this person?

a. A friend who is letting the scoundrel use his address as a cover?

b. Your scoundrel may be renting a room at this address. If so, these landlords know more about their tenants than most, since they also live with them.

A LANDLORD WHO DOES NOT LIVE THERE If the tax bills go to another address, and there is no homeowner's exemption, then this is probably a rental property. In any case, landlords are always good sources of information.

4. If you haven't found him yet, take the full name, driver's license number (from traffic court) or the date of birth, (found on a marriage license, voter's registration or traffic ticket) and send it, or take it, to your local or state Department of Motor Vehicles along with your case number and the name of the court where you got your judgment. *(In California, don't bother. This is the first state, perhaps among many to close their records to the public.)* If, in your state the records are considered public, they will give you the last address your scoundrel gave when he got his latest traffic ticket or had his driver's license renewed. It will probably not be over two years old. If he has moved to another state, the DMV will tell you where he requested that his license be transferred to.

This information is a good source because people have so little control over this aspect of their lives. Most of us, scoundrels included, don't like to lie to a man who wears a gun on his hip.

60

5. Check out the address. To see if the chicken has flown the coop, talk to...

THE NEW RESIDENTS
When did he leave?
Does he still receive mail there? (This tells you if there is a forwarding address on file.)

THE NEIGHBORS
When did he leave?
Who was he friendly with?
Where did he work?
Did he make several trips when moving, and how long did it take him to return between trips. (By this you can tell if he moved a short distance or out of state.)

Size up the people you are talking to. Are they friends? Fellow scoundrels? Or were they also, perchance, taken to the cleaners by this slime? And would they like a friendly shoulder to cry on?

6. Check with the post office. Send one dollar to the local post office of the scoundrel, addressed: Postmaster, Freedom of Information Act, Anytown, MD, Zip. Request the forwarding address of said scoundrel. Many stupid scoundrels fall for the old forwarding address trick.

7. If you haven't found him yet, check with...

OLD PLACES OF BUSINESS: Talk to the boss, personnel department and the office gossip.

RELATIVES: Find them in the assessor's office, voter's registration, or the phone directory.

DEPARTMENT OF MOTOR VEHICLES: This time do an "alpha search," (an alphabetical search, by name and area) for any cars that are registered under the name.

CLUBS: Contact any he might be associated with. Maybe he's a social scoundrel.

UNIONS: They won't give you much information, but they will tell you if he's registered with them, and perhaps if he is still in the area. They will also, most likely, forward a letter to him, but if you think he's going to answer it, you haven't been listening.

NEIGHBORHOOD MERCHANTS: You might get lucky. These guys tend to remember people who give them bad checks.

REGISTERED LETTER: Send him a registered letter at his last address. If he picks it up in person, then you know he is still in the area. If a friend or relative picks it up, then you know that person knows where he is and you just have to come up with the proper scam. Keep reading...

NEIGHBORING COUNTIES: Check their public records and directories.

If all this fails, consider the alternative. He's dead. In which case, remember...living is the best revenge.

PRIVATE MAIL BOXES

The most effective and commonly used way a scoundrel hides his address is through the use of a private mailing company. These addresses appear as street addresses and have, up until now, been considered uncrackable by skiptracers.

I can't tell you how many times I have rushed off to a scoundrel's "new" address only to find that it belonged to a company that rents private mail boxes. It was obvious when I gazed into that little 3" by 4" box, that it was too tiny for even the most petite scoundrel.

And that's why I stopped the presses when I learned this bit of news...

Private mailbox companies must file a form called the *"Application of Delivery of Mail Through an Agent"* with the United States Postal Service for every person or business that rents a mailbox from them. This information is verified by the Postmaster and available only to postal inspectors and law enforcement officers.

However, when I queried the Postmaster, he confirmed that the Post Office would honor a subpoena issued by the court where the civil judgment was obtained. What this means is, with a subpoena, you can obtain all the information on the application of an individual or business receiving mail through a private mailbox company! (You cannot actually see the application, but you can ask for any specific piece of information on it.)

Here is what is available on the application...

Name of Box Holder.
Driver's License Number and Expiration date.
Credit Card and Account Number.
Name of the Company.

Nature of the Business.

Home Address of Applicant.

Business Address.

Names of each member whose mail is to be delivered.

Two References, with Addresses.

Where the Fictitious Business Name, Corporation or Trade Name is Registered and the Date of Filing.

And, oh yeah...The post office will also honor a subpoena requesting information about their own post office box holders.

SCAMS

At some point in your search it will become necessary for you to verify your scoundrel's location. Go yourself or send someone, to gather a little info. If you have never met, you'll need a scam.

TELEPHONE SCAM

If your scoundrel is listed with directory assistance, you don't even need to call to verify that he's still here. Ma Bell won't leave a number connected unless someone is there to pay the bill. She's funny that way. (Call anyway, it's fun. And sometimes Ma's a little tardy in getting change of number info to her operators.)

If you think you have a valid number, but the phone is listed in someone else's name, then call and say something like...

Her: Hello.

You: Maddie, is that you?

Her: Maddie's not here.

You: What time will she be back?

Her: Six.

You: Okay. Thanks. Bye. (Or better still...) Do you have a number where I can reach her at work?

Her: It's none of your business.

You: Okay. Thanks. Bye.

THE EMPTY PACKAGE SCAM

When I go in person I usually take a package of some sort. First off, I think it's rude to show up at someone's home empty-handed. Second, hardly anyone refuses a nicely wrapped empty box. Especially if they think there might be something in it.

THE FULL PACKAGE SCAM

You might even add a little something to the box to give it some weight. Stemware is nice. But don't get too fancy. It makes it hard on the rest of us. In either case, it's best to beat a hasty retreat after you have delivered your package. Unless, of course, it's something really nice.

THE FLOWER SCAM

I used to give flowers, but that got pretty expensive. If you don't find the guy right away they get a little droopy, and then he won't take them even when you do find him.

Girls seem to like them though...

CHARLIE'S SCOUNDREL

Maddie Bunshee was the slimiest kind of scoundrel. She had rented an apartment from a nice couple and then taken advantage of their trusting nature.

I was told Maddie was about 5'6", 33 years old, had a great personality and was bordering on gorgeous. Isn't it amazing how many scoundrels would make a great first date?

Anyway, Maddie had fallen on hard times, her rent accruing faster than she could scam the funds to pay it. On top of that, she had borrowed a couple of grand from her new friends and then split.

I ran Maddie through my normal paces at the county courthouse and came up with an address in Sausalito. A check with the assessor's office proved that the property was owner-occupied.

I showed up in the middle of the day when I knew the owners would probably be away. Through the neighbors, I learned that the owner of the house had lived there for a long time. The assessor's office showed that the property had only one unit. So either Maddie had a friend, or she'd struck again.

I also learned that the owner had a holistic food shop down on the waterfront. Something told me that this would be her connection to Maddie.

I arrived just as the fog crawled over the lush Marin headlands...

The joint was closed, but the boutique next door was open. I went in with my flowers and asked if Maddie Bunshee worked next door. Suddenly, this head of blonde curls popped up in the dressing cubicle in the back. When I exited the store, the curls followed...

CURLS: Are those for Maddie Bunshee?

R.D.D.:   Yes, they are. Are you Maddie Bunshee?

CURLS: No.

R.D.D.:   Do you know Maddie Bunshee?

CURLS: No. Who are the flowers from?

R.D.D.:   I don't know. There's a card, but I would have to give that to Maddie personally.

CURLS: Well, I know someone who might know Maddie. You could just leave them with me.

R.D.D.:   Oh, I'd get in a lot of trouble if I did that. I guess I'll just take them back with me. They'll look nice on my kitchen table.

And so I did. It's a real shame too, because that girl was a dead ringer for Maddie Bunshee.

67

THE NOT YET READY
FOR PRIME-TIME SCOUNDREL

The good thing about THE FLOWER SCAM is that people are just so darn glad to see you.

I once went to an apartment complex with some very nice gladiolus. Gladiolus are my favorite because they are cheap. They are also kind of classy, but I mainly like them because they are cheap. Yet they don't look cheap, like daisies do.

Anyway, I had been through the county courthouse and I knew a lot about Butch Hoffer. I knew, for example, that he had been through a divorce about ten years before, had a couple of kids, and that he paid child support. I also knew that he and his wife, "2-2" (honest injun') once owned property in Oregon. In the divorce settlement, she got it.

When I talked to the manager of the apartment, she confirmed that Butch was gone, but she showed me his rental application so I could get the gladiolus to him before they wilted any more.

On his application, he had listed 2-2 as the next of kin, although they had been divorced for almost ten years. That, to me, indicated they were still chummy. The manager of the apartment complex then added that Butch (he wasn't a scoundrel, he was a witness in a lawsuit) had left so suddenly that he hadn't even picked up his $40 cleaning deposit.

The key was his apparent close relationship with his ex. So I checked with the Oregon operator and, sure enough, *Hoffer, 2-2.*, was listed. I called and told her that I was calling from the apartment complex (which I was) and that the complex still owed Butch his $40 cleaning fee (which they did) and that if she would give me Butch's address I'd have the money sent (which I did).

Another happy ending. The Butch got $40 and an all-expense paid trip back to California. The attorney got his witness. His client won the case. And I got some very nice gladiolus.

WHEN NOT TO USE THE FLOWER SCAM

The important thing to remember in choosing a scam is to approach the subject in a non-threatening way with an offer they can't refuse. Usually flowers are non-threatening. But not always.

I don't do flowers much anymore. But when I did, I had a cute little white coat I used to wear that said, "R.D.D. Delivery" on it.

One day I delivered some roses (they were on "special") to a woman whose large angry husband met me at the door. He looked like the type of guy who hadn't sent roses to his wife in years, and you could tell it kind of ticked him off that somebody else was doing it. I never really knew what happened to that woman, but I never had to go after her again.

Another time I tried to deliver some flowers to a man who had died a couple of years before. This upset the family a lot, and kicked off a kind of impromptu memorial service.

So remember, when choosing a gift, take the time to get to know your scoundrel. Try not to get generic gifts. They can backfire.

7

How To Get The Money

WE'VE GOT MADDIE BUNSHEE!!!!

> *Yes. It's true. The same Maddie Bunshee whose been eluding creditors, attorneys and gumshoes all over the state of California.*
> *But now Rat Dog's got her!*
> *And in this special one-time offer, we'll throw her in for nothing when you order ten more scoundrels at the regular price.*
>
> Advertisement

Tracking down money is like tracking down a person. The money does not just disappear, any more than a person does. Even if your scoundrel dies, you can still find the grave. And if he sells his house, the money still exists in some form. True, it might not be real property anymore, but it still exists somewhere.

71

The trick is to not accept a dead end as the end of the line. Keep searching until you find out what happened to the money.

SCOUNDREL IN LA LA LAND

If there was ever a case where I had to use every trick known to rat dogs to collect a debt, it would be the case of Frank Maddox.

Frank Maddox is the fictitious name of a real life pro-football player, turned B-actor, turned B-producer, turned A-1 scoundrel.

My client had given Frank the best $250,000 of his money. Frank was supposed to use it to finance a movie called "Rambo in Watts" or something. Anyway, that was the last my client ever saw of his investment. My client fell for it because Frank was such a well known personality. His picture was plastered all over billboards. He did guest shots at football games. And there was always some blurb in Variety about his latest he-man adventure.

When Frank never even sent a thank you note for the loot, it was cause for worry. When he didn't respond to phone calls, it was cause for concern. But when he didn't show up in court, it was downright infuriating. Unopposed, my client got a $300,000 judgment...the loan, interest and attorney's fees.

This is the case every detective dreams of. The guy is so high profile that you just know that you can find the money. The bounty is high, and therefore, so is the commission.

And so I took off for Southern California on a combination camping and scoundrel-chasing adventure.

Here's what happened...

From the Department of Motor Vehicles, I learned

that several expensive cars were registered to Maddox. I just had to locate them and tow them away.

Vital Statistics: Marriage license for Frank and Mary Maddox. Married in 1963. Dates of birth and physical descriptions of both. Occupation for Frank; pro-football.

A check with the Assessor's Office showed that Frank owned no property in Los Angeles County. He and his wife, Mary, had owned a tasteful spot in Westwood, but alas, no longer. He had also owned a complex of apartments and shops in Van Nuys, but all that had been sold too.

In the Recorder's Office I found out who the property was sold to, when, and for how much. Might they still owe him money?

There was also a promissory note from a woman who leased a shop from Frank on the Van Nuys property. The note was for $36,000, and it was two years old. There was a good chance something was left on it.

In the County Clerk's Office I found out that my client wasn't Frank's only victim. There were no less than thirteen judgments filed against him in the past ten years. And all for the same thing, taking money from investors and then neglecting to produce a film. All cases were ignored by Maddox. Several of the judgments were vacated when the plaintiff tried to collect on them. Not one was satisfied. Many of Frank's investors were out-of-state. Apparently he knew that these cases were more costly to prosecute and more difficult to collect.

There were several files which were not accessible. They were filed in various sub-county offices. One was Frank and Mary's recent divorce. This is about the best news a collections detective can get. I made a note to go there later.

73

Next, I went to the library of the Motion Picture Academy. His clip file chronicled every little nugget of Frank's public life. There was his first TV job as the hunk/boyfriend of a well-known singer making her acting debut. There was a string of B-movies in the early seventies. Most disgusting of all was a three-page spread in Ebony Magazine where Frank, draped in girls, espoused about what fun it was to be a sex symbol. Where was Mary during all this? Bound up in the leopard drapes with a gag in her mouth?

Frank's clip file also showed that, although he'd made many announcements of coming attractions, Frank had not actually made a film in 13 years!

I could hardly wait to get to Glendale, the county sub-office that held the end of the Frank and Mary love story.

There is no vengeance like a woman scorned: Mary listed, wanted, and got half of all of Frank's yachts, farm equipment, gold coins, property , cars, cash, checking, savings, and insurance policies.

Good for you, Mary! I just want what's left.

Because this was a very large judgment, I really wanted to get my hands on the proceeds from his L.A. real estate holdings. So I did something I had never tried before. In the past, if a property was sold, I just wrote it off. Another fish that got away. But there was a lot of dough riding on this one. And besides, I thought Frank Maddox was slime. Kitty litter. Potting soil. Pond scum.

I called the attorney I was working with and had him subpoena the escrow files from the company that handled the transaction. They were mad as heck, but in the end they had no choice but to comply. We had a judgment against their client, and the judgment entitled us to pursue collection with the help of the court.

74

There was one specific piece of information that I wanted from that thick file. The bank in which Frank's share of the money was deposited. (Even if the money had been moved, we could continue to subpoena bank records until we tracked it down.)

We got the information, but before we could get the writ of execution to the bank, Frank's attorney stepped in. It was his fault, not Frank's, he told the judge, that this lawsuit against Frank had not been contested. Please, he pleaded, do not penalize Frank for the mistake of his attorney.

I'll never quite believe that the judge bought this garbage. The fact that there were 13 judgments against Frank in Los Angeles County for the same scam was not even admissible in court.

The judge vacated the judgment, and not only could we not collect, but the entire case had to be retried.

REAL PROPERTY

Real property is defined as land and improvements owned by an individual, persons or a company. It is one of the easiest sources of assets to locate and one of the hardest to collect on. Whether you want to pursue it or not depends upon the size of your judgment. At the very least, you should place an abstract judgment in that county so that when the property is sold, your claim will be satisfied. Your other options are to either force a sale on the property, or to collect any revenues from it.

But first, let's talk about how to find it...

THE ASSESSOR'S OFFICE

Real property is listed in the County Assessor's Office under the subject's name. To check for real property, call, write or go to each office where you think your scoundrel might have property. Check the county where he lives, surrounding counties, and any other counties where he might have vacation property. Check all counties if you are thorough or desperate. In some counties there exists a separate index for commercial and residential property. Be sure you check both.

Check the index under:
> The subject's name
> The company name
> Any corporation names
> The spouse's name
> Any other names on your judgment

If you find a listing for property, you'll need the following information from the assessor's office.

NAME Are properties listed in his name, or in a joint ownership, or in a company name?

MAILING ADDRESS The mailing address can contain clues as to other counties or states in which to check for property. Also, perhaps a business address is listed. If it is an unfamiliar address, then check it out.

SITUS ADDRESS The actual location of the property.

ASSESSOR'S PARCEL NUMBER Note it. You'll need it in order to identify any other transactions in the Recorder's Office.

ASSESSOR'S VALUE Notoriously low. This reflects the buyer's price plus a certain percentage each year. The earlier the property was bought, and the greater the appreciation in your area, the greater the discrepancy between the assessor's value and the actual appraised value.

HOMEOWNER'S EXEMPTION California lists $7,000 as a homeowner's exemption. If it is claimed, it means the subject lives at this address. In some states, on an owner-occupied property, a sale cannot be forced in order to satisfy a debt other than that of the mortgage.

ZONE USAGE Ask the assessor what the code means. Is it a single family dwelling, duplex, condo, commercial property or offices? Keep in mind that any rental property income can be garnished.

BASE YEAR/DOCUMENT NUMBER The assessor sometimes lists this information. It will help you locate the deed. On the deed you will find the purchase price as well as any mortgages listed against the property.

If your scoundrel has property...

Check with the assessor as to the date that the index was compiled. Ask him if he has the latest listings. If not, check in the Grantor/Grantee Index in the County Recorder's Office. You will want the information dated after the assessor compiled his index.

77

RECORDER'S OFFICE

DEED Was the property sold since the assessor's index was compiled?

TRUSTEE'S SALE Was the property sold because your scoundrel couldn't make the payments?

NOTICE OF INTENT OF SALE Is he about to lose the property? If so, there may still be time to get your bid in. File an abstract judgment immediately. This, however, is not a good sign. If he's losing his home in a trustee's sale, he's broke. Don't expect a pot full of money somewhere else.

QUIT CLAIM Did your scoundrel sign the property over to someone else? If the Quit Claim was signed before you got your judgment, then you're sunk. If it was deeded after, then it's time for an attorney. You may have a legal right to attach it, but it could involve another lawsuit to prove it. (Isn't this fun?)

If the property passes all these tests, then you'll need to determine whether it has enough equity in it to justify going to the expense of forcing a sale.

ANY EQUITY IN THE PROPERTY?

Look for...

DEED OF TRUST/ASSIGNMENT OF RENTS OR MORT-GAGE (DT/AR) (Where your subject is the grantor.) This document records any loans which list the property as collateral. It could be issued by a bank or a private party, or by the previous owner of the property. The initial mortgage will be recorded with the deed. Be sure that the document refers to the property in question. Do this by comparing the Assessor's Parcel Numbers. (APN)

These documents will be filed any time from the date of the trust deed to the present. Is it recent? If so, there is probably still a balance due your scoundrel. Obviously, the older the document, the smaller the balance of payments and the more equity in the property.

RECONVEYANCE   (Where your subject is the grantee.) When the DT/AR is paid off, the homeowner (grantee) is issued a reconveyance.   It's like getting "paid" stamped on your layaway bill.

ABSTRACT JUDGMENTS   If your subject is a true scoundrel, you won't be the only one he owes money to. Judgment creditors, like you, will file an abstract judgment so that any property he owns will have a cloud on the title. Judgments are paid out of the sale of the property on a first-come-first-serve basis.

MECHANIC'S LIENS   These are filed by contractors claiming an outstanding balance for work done on the property. If they were recorded before you recorded your claim on the property, they are in line ahead of you.

HOMESTEAD   This document protects the scoundrel's primary place of residence against a forced sale by a judgment creditor.

79

HOW TO INTERPRET YOUR FINDINGS

TRUSTEE'S SALE OR QUIT CLAIM In either case, you are out of luck. Unless it looks like your scoundrel quit-claimed in order to avoid paying on your judgment, forget it. If it looks like he did, check with your attorney. You might have to go back to court to prove it. Only you can decide if it's worth it.

PROPERTY STILL OWNED, HOMEOWNER'S EXEMPTION CLAIMED The chances of forcing a sale on a primary residence (whether protected with a homestead or not) differs from state to state. In California, for example, forget it. Wipe it out of your mind, it's not going to happen. The only judgment /creditors who can consistently upset a homestead are the federal and state tax collectors (natch) and the mortgage holder of the property.

PROPERTY STILL OWNED, LIENS ON TITLE   To determine the equity in a property, take the assessed value (either from the purchase price plus inflation, or from a realtor's appraisal) and subtract the liens on the property. What's left, if anything, is called equity.

Now...

1. File an abstract judgment to assure that your claim is next in line, and that the property cannot be sold without satisfying your claim.

2. Obtain a writ of execution from the court and deliver it, along with written instructions to the levying officer, (usually the sheriff) directing him to levy against the property.

3.   The levying officer will then serve a copy of the levy to the astonished and chagrined scoundrel. He will also legally record it and serve a notice to the occupants of the property. If the property is unoccupied, he will post the notice on the front door.

4.   File an application with the court for an order of sale on the dwelling. This must be done immediately or the property will be released from the lien.

5.   Follow the sheriff's instructions. Eventually the property will be sold at an auction. The minimum bid must exceed the amount of the homeowner's exemption, plus any liens on the property. If no bid is acceptable, the property will be released and cannot be sold for another year. If this happens, many times you will be unable to recover the expense of forcing the sale. You can, however, come up with the minimum bid yourself, using the full amount of your judgment as a credit bid.

PROPERTY SOLD Drat! Despair, but do not give up hope. Check the deed for the escrow office and the number of the transaction. Failing that, get the name of the title company and then ask them for the escrow office.

Next, have your attorney subpoena the entire escrow file from the escrow office. He'll need the name of the seller of the property, the file number and the witness fee (usually under $25.) Expect the fur to fly. Escrow offices pride themselves on privacy, and they hate it when someone outsmarts them and forces their hand.

When you get the file, it will contain the canceled check from the new buyer of the property. It will be made out to your scoundrel and deposited in his account. Now you not only have *a* bank account number, you have *the* bank account number! Not the one with the grocery money in it, but the one with the real loot.

The next step is to file a notice of levy against the account. Most scoundrels, although they know that you have subpoenaed the file (not only are most escrow officers awful snitches, but the court informs the scoundrel as well) they won't have a clue as to why you did it.

If the account has been closed by the time you get there, just subpoena that bank's records. Along with his bank application, you'll find all kinds of other information, like which bank the money was transfered to! If that bank comes up dry, go through the same procedure. Unless he walked out with it in a paper sack, you will find the money.

RENTAL PROPERTY

You should already, from your trip to the Assessor's Office, have an idea as to the extent of your scoundrel's real estate holdings. All property, aside from his own home, is likely to be rental income. You can force a sale on these properties, but you might not want to.

Why not? Perhaps there is not enough equity in the property. Perhaps there are so many abstract judgments, mortgages or mechanic's liens in line in front of you that it would be pointless.

In any case, it could be far more profitable, and

expedient to file a writ of attachment requesting that the renter send his rent money to you instead of the landlord.

In order to do this, you'll need the name and address of the people writing the rent checks. This can be acquired from the Haines Reverse Directory or the Polk Criss-Cross Directory located in the library of the county where the property is. (You can also sometimes get it from the reference librarian, by phone.) Another method is to check the mailboxes for the tenants' names, or to confide in a sympathetic neighbor. Be sure and get the names of everyone at that property. You don't know who might actually be writing the check.

If the property is managed by a property manager, you're in luck. Simply let him continue to collect the rents, after all, that's his job, and then have the court instruct him to send the checks directly to you. Now you are dealing with just one person instead of individual tenants who might move and complicate your life. Also, the manager, being a businessman himself, will probably be more cooperative with a court order than a confused tenant who may think he'll be evicted if he stops paying the landlord.

HOME RENTALS

Don't neglect to check for legal or illegal units in your scoundrel's own home. Scoundrels, and some of the rest of us as well, have been known to be guilty of this bit of domestic entrepreneuring. Legal second units are listed with the city or county building departments. Illegal second units are listed with the neighbors.

REAL PROPERTY, OTHER COUNTIES

To check for real property owned by the scoundrel in other counties, get a list of all of the county assessor's offices from your own county assessor.
Then write each county assessor asking for any property in the scoundrel's name. In addition, ask for; the situs (location), the mailing address, the assessor's value, the Assessor's Parcel Number (APN) of the property, the zone and usage of the property, and whether the taxpayer has filed a homeowner's exemption.

PROMISSORY NOTES & DEEDS OF TRUST/ ASSIGNMENT OF RENTS

This document is recorded in the County Recorder's Office. They are also called Mortgages, Second Mortgages or Carry Back Loans.

When your scoundrel is the grantor, it means he is the one who is paying the money. When he is the grantee, however, it means that he is the recipient or beneficiary of the money.

There are two reasons why your scoundrel might be the beneficiary of a Deed of Trust/Assignment of Rents. Most likely, your scoundrel sold a property and provided financing. In this case it will be filed with the Deed of Trust at the time of the sale.

It could also mean that he regularly invests in DT/ARs, which would obviously yield a higher interest rate than other investments.

To find these loans, go through the Grantor/ Grantee Index in the County Recorder's Office. Go back at least fifteen years. When interest loans skyrocketed several years ago and no-money-down plans became popular, a lot of sellers took carry-back loans in order to sell their property. (See *Where to Find the Dough*" for a further and even more confusing explanation of the Grantor/Grantee Index.) The amount of the loan will be on the document, the terms normally are not. Check for any reconveyances or satisfaction of mortgages that correspond to these documents. It could be that the loan has already been paid off.

Should you find a Deed of Trust/Assignment of Rents, send a garnishment to the person who is paying off the loan.

EMPLOYMENT

Finding out where someone works is either the easiest or the hardest kind of information to get. I find it difficult because I am so shy.

I know of no way to find out where someone works simply by going through public records. Voter's registration may list an occupation, but never an employer. This is, of course, some help, especially if that occupation is a profession that is registered and regulated by the state. Usually the most effective way to find out a place of employment is...THE SCAM!

JURY DUTY SCAM

By telephone...

Curls: Hello.

R.D.:   Maddie Bunshee, please.

Curls: Who's this?

R.D.:   I'm calling from the Marin County Jury Duty Department. I'm calling to inform you of your turn for jury duty next week.

Curls: Oh c'mon! I'm not even registered to vote!

R.D.:   That's an outdated theory, Miss Bunshee. Nowadays jurors are chosen from assessor's rolls, business licenses and... (name some list you know Maddie's on.)

Curls: Damn!

R.D.:   Miss Bunshee, please! Anyway, not to worry. There are legitimate reasons for avoiding jury duty. Do you have a job where your presence is required for the next two months?

Curls: Uh...yeah, I do!

R.D.:   Okay. Just give me your place of employment. We'll list it on this form, and hopefully that will be the end of it.

Curls: Great! I work at Staple Recyclers of America.

R.D.:   We'll have to verify that. Address?

THE MELTING
CHOCOLATE EASTER BUNNY SCAM

For the landlord

R.D.:   Hello. Is this Arty Funkmire?

Arty: Yes, it is.

R.D.:   Hi. I'm calling from Kisses 'N Kandy. I'm wondering if you can help me.

Arty: Talk to me.

R.D.:   I have a giant chocolate bunny rabbit (or other appropriate holiday gift) that I've had in my trunk for almost a week. I keep trying to get it delivered to Maddie Bunshee, but she's never home. You own that property at 234 Elm, right?

Arty: Yeah.

R.D.:   Well, I've got to get this bunny delivered. His ears are starting to droop. Can you give me a work address or phone for her?

Arty: Oh sure. She works at Staple Recyclers of America. I don't know the address, but it's in the book.

R.D.:   Okay. Great. Thanks. Bye.

   If the neighbor doesn't know where Maddie works, try for the time she leaves for work so you can "catch her at home" (aka "follow her to work.")

OLD FRIEND SCAM

For the neighbors...

R.D.: Hi. My name is Rat Dog Dick. I have a friend whom I haven't seen in a while...Maddie Bunshee, next door? Anyway, I just went over there and I guess she's moved.

O.G.*: Yeah. About a year ago.

R.D.: You don't know where I can find her, do you? I have to take a plane out tonight, so I guess I'll need a work number or I'll never catch up with her.

O.G.: Gosh, I don't know where she works.

R.D.: Was there someone in the neighborhood who she was friendly with?

O.G.: Yeah. The Schwartzes over at 125.

R.D.: Great. Thanks. Bye.

*Other Guy

Note: Pick the logical one for your friend. Not the scoundrel himself perhaps, but the wife or one of the kids. If you try this scam on the phone and they want a return number so they can call you back, explain that you are at a pay phone, and the number isn't on it.

COLLECTION

After you locate the place of employment, the court will give you a wage garnishment form to fill out. This will be sent to the scoundrel's employer, and up to 25% of his wages will be attached and sent to you. The percentage of the garnishment will differ from state to state, but the point is to leave him enough so that he won't stop working.

As with other liens, you could be in line behind other wage garnishrs. They will be taken in consecutive order. Child and spousal support attachments are given priority.

THE BAD NEWS

Again, expect the courts to bend over backwards to protect the scoundrel. Just when you've worked so hard to locate his assets and levy against them, the scoundrel seems to get a reprieve.

The culprit is the *"Claim of Exemption,"* a court order that allows the debtor to keep any personal property that is considered a basic necessity. This personal property can extend to his wages as well, effectively protecting them from garnishment. This means that you can't even get the 25%. He does not, however, automatically have these rights, he must petition the court for them.

BUSINESS INCOME

Another obvious source of income is the revenue from any businesses that your scoundrel owns, or has part ownership in. Businesses can be owned by...

89

SOLE OWNERSHIP When a business is owned by one person, any income from that business is considered his personal income and is fair game.

PARTNERSHIP When the business is owned by two or more people, part of the income from that business can be attached. If your scoundrel is on salary, then his wages can be attached. Expect him to be less than candid about his income, since he is both the boss and the employee.

CORPORATIONS If the business is a corporation and the judgment is only against the individual, then no assets of the corporation can be attached. If the judgment is against the corporation, then they can be.

WHERE TO GET
INFORMATION ON BUSINESSES

SECRETARY OF STATE Corporations are listed with the Secretary of State, or the Corporation Commission or some equivalent, in the capital city of each state. In some states, they are not indexed by owners' name, only by the corporate name. Records could also list the amount of stock that your scoundrel owns in the company.

SECURITY AND EXCHANGE COMMISSION If the corporation is publicly owned, and the stock is sold on the open market, it will be listed with the SEC. Regional offices are in New York, Boston, Atlanta, Chicago, Fort Worth, Denver and Los Angeles. The SEC regulates securities traded on the thirteen national exchanges, as well as investigate any possible cases of fraud. All this is public record. Any company with more than 500 stockholders and more than one million dollars in assets is required to file a public annual report.

FICTITIOUS BUSINESS NAME INDEX Located in the County Clerk's Office, this is a listing of all unincorporated companies doing business in the county. Still, your scoundrel might not be listed here. Why not? Because he's a sleazeball, that's why! Actually, the only reason I've ever found for listing a business in the Fictitious Business Name Index is to facilitate cashing checks made out in the company name. If a business is listed, it will include the owners' names, addresses of the owners at the time of the filing, phone numbers, the type and physical location of the business.

BUSINESS LICENSES Located in City Hall are licenses for businesses operating within the city limits. Usually they are restaurants and shops. The records are public and may or may not be indexed according to the owner's name, depending upon the county. City clerks, however, can be quite helpful in recalling who are their up-and-coming or down-and-outing businessmen. Applications will contain names, addresses and phone numbers of both the business and the owner, as well as the type of business.

UNSECURED TAX ROLLS Located in the Tax Assessor's Office at the County Courthouse. Taxes levied on businesses are sometimes considered public record, depending upon the county. The information you will find here can be anything from a frustrating lead to a gold mine. At worst, it can tell you that your scoundrel is involved in a business and that business' name. At best, it will tell you what he claimed the company was worth the previous year.

91

NEWSPAPER MORGUE You can find the back issues of both local and major metropolitan newspapers in your county library. You can also find past issues at the newspaper office itself. If the business has had any publicity at all, there will be a record of it in the newspaper. It might also be worth a call to the advertising department, once you locate a company name.

PROFESSIONAL LICENSING BOARD Located in the capitol city of your state, professional businesses are registered and regulated by the state. Any attorney, doctor, bar-owner, or beautician will be listed under his own name. The regulatory board will also give you the owner's name, business name, address, phone number and whether or not the license is in good standing. (See "Specialized Services" under *"Where to Find the Dough."*)

WHOLESALERS' RESALE APPLICATION Businesses that sell to retail outlets are exempt from paying sales tax if they file an application for a wholesaler's resale license. State regulations differ as to whether this information is available to the public, but it's worth checking.

WHEN YOU DON'T KNOW WHERE TO GO

If you have a career field for your scoundrel but can't find a business name, try this. Call someone out of the yellow pages listed in the field you are investigating. Ask them if a government agency regulates their industry and who you should contact to find or investigate a company or individual. Be truthful with them and you will probably find them helpful. If they're not, hang up and call someone else.

COLLECTING ON BUSINESS INCOME

If your scoundrel is the proud owner of a working viable business where money arrives in the mail or via walk-in traffic, contact the sheriff's office about putting a "till" on the business. He will set up a little desk near the cash register and save the cashier the bother. You can keep him there until the judgment is fully collected. Sometimes just the sight of the sheriff carrying his little tin box is enough to make a scoundrel think twice about paying off that judgment.

If it is a home business...say your scoundrel sells cement mixers door-to-door, try another approach. Arrange, or have a friend arrange, to put a down payment on a mixer. When the check is cashed, you'll find out which account the money is deposited in. Then you can put a levy on the account.

Another avenue is to find someone who has received a check from your scoundrel already (a supplier, landlord, etc.) and get the account number from them. There is one drawback here...the supplier could contact the scoundrel. To avoid this, get the information from someone who is also a victim. A good source of this information is the Plaintiff/Defendant's Index at the County Clerk's Office.

WHAT DO YOU MEAN THIS BUSINESS HAS NO MONEY?

Yes, Virginia, it's true. Businesses don't need bank accounts anymore. They can just charge against a line of credit provided by their bank, and then pay it off in cash. And so, businesses can run, completely legally, without a checking account. And, unfortunately, there is no way you can collect on it because you can't attach credit.

BANK ACCOUNTS

A bank account is probably the most difficult asset to locate. Ironically, it is the easiest to collect on.

BANK CONTACT

I have a friend who works in the computer room of one of a large bank. He claims in order to access account information, the operator must punch in his personal code number to identify himself. This kind of activity, unauthorized, would put not only his job, but his entire career in jeopardy. I cannot see this as a contact that one could easily cultivate.

However, private investigators routinely run "computer checks" to locate bank accounts. God only knows who these sources are, but I must say - if a person has an account in their own name, these guys can find it.

The cost? About 200 balloons. But if they fail, kiss your balloons goodbye. (Lots of scoundrels don't have bank accounts.) And don't come crying to me.

THROUGH THE BACK DOOR

The best way I know to get a bank account number (without paying for it) is to trace it through another source.

Tracking money is like tracking down a person. With a person, you will find one of two things at the end of the line, a live person, or a dead person. But with money, it might start out as a house in the country, turn into a cashier's check, change into mutual funds, get halved in a divorce, and end up at the race track. The important thing to remember is, once you get a line on the loot, don't get thrown when it changes form.

Your most powerful weapon here is the power of the subpoena. You have a right to use it because you hold a judgment against the debtor. Too often the creditor overlooks this legal tool, and spends his time trying to trick silly little bank tellers, only to find out they're not silly at all. Why do this when you can, by law, make them tell you where the money is?

MUNICIPAL & SUPERIOR COURT FILES

In your research, you should make note of any canceled checks that you come across. Sometimes these checks are merely an exhibit of insufficient funds, but it's worth a call to the bank to find out. Even if there is no canceled check in the file, the plaintiff in the case is worth talking to. I've found them to be very helpful. Exchange information with them or simply commiserate. Offer to share your scoundrel's dwindling fortune, should you find anything.

Even if the plaintiff no longer has his cancelled check, you can still find out which bank the check was drawn on. Most depositors list the AB transit number on their deposit slip, along with the amount of the check. If they no longer have a copy of the deposit slip, they can request one from the bank.

Here's how to decode an AB transit number.

AB TRANSIT NUMBER

$$\frac{68\text{-}1}{510}$$

ABOVE THE LINE The first two numbers identify the city or state where the bank is located. If the number is from 1 to 49, it is a city; if it is from 50 to 99, it represents a state. The second number identifies the bank. Any bank in your area will translate this number for you.

BELOW THE LINE The first number tells you which Federal Reserve District the bank is located. The numbers go from 1 to 12. The middle number distinguishes between the head or branch office of the Federal Reserve District. The third number is credit information.

You should be concerned primarily with the numbers above the line, as they represent the city and bank where the check originated. You will be charged for every writ you send, regardless of whether the account has been closed, or has any funds in it, but, should you collect, the charges you have paid can be added to your judgment.

RUSES, PRETEXTS AND LIES

Many private investigators count on tricking the scoundrel into telling them where they bank. Either the investigators are very good, or their scoundrels are very stupid. I am so used to dealing with hard-core scoundrels that I cannot believe they would fall for some of the stuff that I've read about in detective manuals. However, if you have a low-grade scoundrel, you might want to try one of these.

THE ELECTRIC COMPANY RUSE Call the scoundrel and say that you are from the electric company and unless they pay their bill immediately, you are going to turn off their power. When they protest, offer to check further. Ask what bank the check was drawn on, make some computer noises, admit your error, apologize profusely, tell them to have a nice day and hang up.

BANK SOLICITATION PRETEXT Call the scoundrel from a "new" bank, (R.D.D. Savings and Loan) and offer him a free checking account as a promotional offer. When he says he is not interested, ask where he now banks, thank him and hang up. (I told you these were stupid.)

THE CHECK'S IN THE MAIL LIE Mail a check from a business account where the scoundrel has had no contact, along with a form letter stating that he has been overcharged for some type of service. When the scoundrel deposits the check in his bank, it will come back in your statement with his bank and account number on the back of the check. This is a good plan, but hard-core scoundrels know about it.

GETTING INFORMATION FROM A BANK

Banks are really touchy about who they give account information out to. Ironically, the two pieces of identification that banks normally asks for to verify a caller's identity are his date of birth and his mother's maiden name, both of which can be found on his marriage license, on public record at the County Courthouse or State Vital Statistics Office.

COLLECTION

As I said before, bank accounts are the easiest form of assets to collect on. Go back to the court where you obtained the judgment, get a Writ of Attachment and give it to a private process server. Tell them to hold it until you give him the go-ahead. Then call the bank every day and ask if a check for the amount of the judgment will clear. Keep calling and coming down in the amount until you determine how much is in the account. Monitor the account for about a month and when it reaches the highest plateau, have the process server serve the Writ of Attachment.

Do not give it to the sheriff to serve. If you do, you will have no control over when they send it to the bank. This makes it a crap shoot. There may be $2,000 in the account one day and nothing the next.

STOCKS

Stocks are good, collectable income. The problem is, how do you know if your scoundrel has stock, and where is it?

You can, in theory send a garnishment to each

98

of the top brokerage firms in your town just to query them, and determine if your scoundrel has stock there. But that costs money and is time consuming. And the longer it takes, the better the chance that the stocks will no longer be there when the garnishment finally comes down.

Here's a scam that will help you sort through the maze of brokerages.

Call around to the top brokerage firms in your city. Do it about noon when the scoundrel's broker is probably "doing lunch." Tell the receptionist that you are the brother or sister of the scoundrel and say that you were told to call the firm, but you've forgotten the broker's name. Can they check it, and put you through to your brother's rep? Once you get the name, you know that your scoundrel has stock at that branch and the name of his rep. If you should get through to the broker, click your phone, explain that you have call waiting, and that you'll get back to him. Then don't.

TRUST FUNDS

To locate income from a trust fund or will, go to the County Clerk's Office and check the Probate Index, sometimes listed in the Plaintiff/Defendant's Index, and sometimes listed separately. Look for the last name of your scoundrel, but not his first name. We're looking for his dead, and preferably wealthy relatives. Check with neighboring counties, as well as in his hometown, if you know it.

Should you find nothing in the Probate Index, it could mean several things. First, maybe you are looking in the wrong county. Second, maybe no one died and left anything to your scoundrel. Third, maybe the deceased had a different last name than your scoundrel. Of course, you have to consider that your subject is a scoundrel. The guy who died might not like him any better than you do. In which case, he might be the only one in the family to be left a poor relation.

If you feel there is trust money somewhere and you want to research it further, then it is necessary to discover other family names that the probate file might be under. First, check the State Vital Statistic's Index in the County Recorder's Office. If your scoundrel has ever been married in your state, a record of the union will be in the index. The index is listed by both bride and groom, and it will indicate the spouse's name. When you get the wife's maiden name, run it through the probate index.

If you still come up dry, you might want to enlist the aid of an amateur genealogist. They'd probably get a big kick out of helping you.

I would not go through this extended procedure unless I strongly suspected that my subject was the recipient of a will. But if I did know for sure that he had inherited money, I'd follow through on every lead, even checking out the state and county where the scoundrel grew up. You can make an educated guess at this information by comparing the first three numbers of his social security number (available on tax liens at the County Recorder's Office) with the list in the chapter entitled, *"How to Get the Dough."* This will tell you what state the scoundrel was in when he got his social security number.

MOTOR VEHICLES

Cars, boats, and airplanes are easy to find assets. And, if there is enough equity in them, they are fairly simple to collect on.

To locate them, go to your local Department of Motor Vehicles*, or write to the state office in the capital city. Request an "alpha search." This is a computer check, by name, for any vehicles registered to an individual. You should receive a list of vehicles, the address of the registered owner, and the legal owner if the car is not paid off. Next, call the legal owner and ask what is still owed on the vehicle. If you explain that you are a judgment creditor, they will probably give you the information. (*DMV information is not available to the public in every state.)

COLLECTION

In most states, a base amount is exempted from collection on a primary vehicle. This means, on Maddie Bunshee's only car, Maddie will get the first $1,200 (since Maddie's from California) if the car is sold in order to satisfy a debt.

In addition, the legal owner will have to be paid off before you can collect your judgment. You get the rest, minus the $250 or so it takes to have the sheriff haul it away. The sheriff's fee is added to the amount of the judgment so you will be reimbursed for that if you choose to attach the car.

But beware, there better be a lot of equity in the car if you're going to get anything out of it. If Maddie's car is worth $2,500 and Maddie still owes $1,500 on it, the equity is only $1,000. Maddie gets the first $1,200, therefore you're out of luck! Obviously, it's best to figure this out before you put out $250 for the sheriff to tow it.

If you do locate a vehicle worth collecting on, act quickly. In some states, the DMV informs the scoundrel that there has been an inquiry into his registration information. Obviously, any scoundrel with a lick of sense would go out and get himself a locked garage.

However, on the plus side, I've had some of them pay up just because they realize that the collection fairy is upon them. In fact, I've found that Jaguar owners will almost always pay up if they think you've got the hots for their wheels!

Here's the procedure...

1.   Fill out a writ of execution at the sheriff's office. Submit it, along with the fee.

2.   The sheriff goes to the scoundrel's home or business or to wherever you tell him the car is located. If he's home, the sheriff will explain that he has come to take the car in order to sell it and satisfy the judgment. If he is not home, the sheriff will post a copy of the writ on the door.

3.   The sheriff will then either hot-wire the car, or use the scoundrel's keys to take it away.

4.   The car will be stored for ten days. If the scoundrel does not file an appeal for exemption (claiming the car is used for business, etc.) it will be sold at public auction.

5.   The proceeds of the sale are used to pay off the debt. After the legal owner gets his money, and the scoundrel receives the amount of exemption on the car, and the sheriff gets his towing and storage fees...you get what's left. But only up to the amount of the judgment.

REFUNDS AND DEPOSITS

SECURITY DEPOSITS

Security deposits are the property of the person placing the deposit, not the person or institution holding the deposit. That means that you can garnish utility and phone deposits, as well as a security deposit on an office or apartment.

PENSIONS

Some pensions are exempt from collection and some are not. Ask in the law library of your county courthouse, to find out what is garnishable in your state.

PERSONAL PROPERTY

Probably the best kept collection secret of all is the sheriff's demand on personal property. (It's such a good secret that even some sheriffs claim not to know about it!) Some personal property is exempted by state law from being levied against, usually "tools

103

of the trade," that property a person needs in order to go about his daily work.

So how do you go about finding personal property? The best way is to find someone in the know, who will spill the beans. Above and beyond that, you can make some educated guesses. Like get the floor plans of his home from the building department. If he has a wine cellar, then chances are...he has wine.

You must be as specific as possible about identifying an item, if you are to be successful. The sheriff can be personally held libel if he garnishes the wrong property, which is why sheriffs are so reluctant to do this type of collection. You'll have better luck if you have the serial number of a VCR than if you just list, "a VCR."

RHINESTONE SCOUNDREL

One of my first coups was to collect from a fleeing jeweler who had escaped with about $25,000 worth of rings he was appraising for my client.

Via an accident report, I located him in Salinas California. I checked with the Monterey County Fictitious Business Index, as well as with the people who register city business licenses, but there was no listing for George Florez. In fact, there was no listing in any public record for him.

All I had was Florez' address. I had no choice but to do the most unfun kind of investigating there is...surveillance.

I sat outside George's apartment from six a.m. until he went to work at two p.m. (Never have I waited less than three hours for someone to emerge. I'm tempted to say, flat out, that scoundrels never work the morning shift.) Finally George came out, climbed in his car and drove off. By this time I had my seat fully reclined, was munching on twinkies and going over Soap Opera Digest to see if I missed anything.

I almost missed George!

George drove a mile and a half at break-neck speeds, parked in a shopping center parking lot and disappeared. I stumbled across him as he was fiddling with an automatic teller machine.

Bingo! The bank!

From there he strolled into a jewelry store. When he didn't come out in twenty minutes, I figured he wasn't a shopper. I entered and discovered I was right. He was working in a small booth in the back, doing some engraving.

Now I had located a bank, a car and a job for George Florez. But I still wanted to get back my client's jewelry, or at least the equivalent of George's.

I walked up to the small booth where George was engraving. He looked up at me and smiled, pleased at my interest. "Mind if I watch?" I asked. He seemed happy with the attention.

While George worked carefully away, I went to work. I memorized both of his rings, the stones and designs, and made a mental description of his Rolex watch.

A couple of weeks later George went to work as usual. There he got a notice that 25% of his wages were being attached. When he went to lunch, he found his car had gone along without him. When he went to the bank, he discovered he was broke. That night he was greeted by a sheriff who had designs on his diamonds.

I just hope George never reads this book.

WHAT KIND OF STUFF DOES HE HAVE?

When thinking about what qualifies as personal property, the possibilities are endless. Think about what it is that you own and write it down. You will begin to get the picture.

EXEMPTED PROPERTY

Some of your debtor's assets are protected from garnishment. In order to collect personal property, you must know what is exempted by each state.

Check the following..

* Primary Residence: Is it exempt?
* Other Real Property: Can you get it?
* Vehicles: Is there an equity limit that must be met? If the vehicle is used for business, can you still attach it?
* Second Vehicle: Is it fair game?
* Tools of the Trade: Are they garnishable?
* Wages: What percentage is garnishable? Can only one creditor collect at a time?
* Personal Property: Which of it is exempt?

In virtually every state the following are exempted from collection by a judgment creditor...

Life Insurance Policies, Health & Disability Income, Insurance Benefits, Workman's Compensation, Unemployment, Public Assistance, Aid to Dependent Children, Crime Victims Benefits, Wrongful Death Benefits, Social Security Benefits

The court may also make a determination on a case by case basis. If you're not sure, try it. Maybe it will work. And if it doesn't...you're sure to make your scoundrel a nervous wreck anyway.

GETTING NASTY

Scoundrels have to pay some bills or they would not be able to function in society. The trick is to make your bill one that the scoundrel feels he must pay. You do this by making his life sheer hell.

When you are checking for state exemptions, read between the lines.

For example, pets are exempt in some states. Does that mean you can get your scoundrel's family pet if it is not listed as an exemptible item? Sure it does! And puppynapping is a big attention-getter. Now, you might not want three chickens, a rooster, two ferrets and a partridge in a pear tree, but your scoundrel probably does or he wouldn't have them. And unless he's a real cad, he's not going to let you take Bootsie away in a bag.

Try sending the sheriff after the scoundrel's toilet seat cover or his wife's birth control pills. By the time the sheriff gets around to ripping out his carpeting, I'll bet he's willing to settle with you.

Check out the following to see if they are exempt from collection in your state...

Camera, Jewelry, Television, Burial Plots, Church Pews, Wedding Rings, Personal Library, Retirement Plans, Security Deposits, Domestic Animals, Profit Sharing Plans, Video Tape Recorder, State Income Tax Refunds, Fuel for Heating and Cooking

107

Remember...It's not what you want, it's what he wants that counts!

A WORD ABOUT CHILD SUPPORT

Collecting child support is like collecting any other debt except that you do so with the help of the Family Support division of the district attorney's office. Each state (and even county) differs in how much they can help, but almost all appreciate whatever you can do personally to locate your scoundrel-ex and his/her money.

Getting you through the maze of red tape necessary to perform this staggering task takes a whole other book, so let me suggest one. Order *The Handbook on Child Support Enforcement* from the Government Printing office - or, for your convenience - from the back of this book. It's straight from the horses' mouth info on what you can and can't do.

In the meantime, several things you should know about child support.

1.   You must know who the father is. This is not a big revolving fund like welfare. Child support comes from the absent parent, so if you're a little confused as to who fathered your child, you might suggest some DNA testing.

2.   You must find papa or mama yourself. Although the D.A. has locators, their caseload is too heavy for you to rely on them. Your chances are 100% better if you come in with a person rather than with a memory.

3.   You must file your judgment in the county where the absent/scoundrel lives. No judgment can be enforced unless it is registered in the proper county.

Where To Find The Dough

*"With Rat Dog there are no bulky re-
ports to read. Rat Dog just tells you where
they are and where they keep the dough."*
Another satisfied customer

SCOUNDREL A GO-GO

One of my all time favorite scoundrels was Mai
Li Storme.

Mai Li was a beautiful Vietnamese lady whose
sordid past included stints as the madam of a Tenderloin brothel, a North Beach stripper and the co-owner
of a bar on Polk Street.

She had been sued by her former boyfriend/co-
bar owner. Mai Li had accepted his diamonds, money
and Cadillac before she unceremoniously dumped

109

him for a parking lot attendant. Now she was on the lam and the bar owner had a $25,000 judgment against her.

I looked for Mai Li for the better part of a year. I found several judgments against her for diamond rings she'd partially paid for before she disappeared. I knew where she kept the rings. I just couldn't find her fingers.

Okay, I got a little desperate toward the end. I even took to socializing in North Beach dressed like I might be a friend of Mai Li's. I didn't find her, but at least now I know I won't starve if the detective business doesn't work out.

Mai Li's name stopped appearing in the San Francisco County court records about the time I got the case. I figured either Mai Li had gone straight or she'd split town.

Finally, after several fruitless trips to the DMV, I convinced a friendly clerk to do some in-depth checking. The plate of her Cadillac had, for the past six months, been coming back as a "plate in transition." The clerk told me that Mai Li was changing her vanity plate to a regular one, but she had never completed the transaction, and the car had not yet been registered. It seemed no matter how long I waited, Mai Li never got around to re-registering her car...along with her new address.

I talked the clerk into checking further. Yes, indeed, there was another, more recent entry. A traffic ticket out of the Orange County court. However, the computer still listed her home address as the same old dive in San Francisco. With nothing more than a traffic ticket number from an Orange County court, I took off for Southern California.

From there it was too easy to even be interesting. The court gave me Mai Li's address, incredibly just blocks from the courthouse. Most embarrassing of all was the fact that Mai Li, address and all, was listed in the Orange County phone book. She'd been listed there all along, I just didn't know which phone book to look in.

The Alcohol Control Board clerk told me that Mai Li Storme had never applied for a liquor license in L.A. or Orange Counties. From this I determined she was no longer a bar owner.

Early in the morning I cruised Mai Li's house and spotted her Cadillac. Early in the afternoon she finally got in it. We did a little shopping, went to the post office and got a car wash. Then we went to lunch with friends. Hers, not mine.

About three o'clock, Mai Li drove across town and stopped at a seedy tavern. When she stayed longer than it would take for a quick snort, I went in to check it out.

There was dear little Mai Li working her first honest job in ages.

I ended up spending the afternoon with Mai Li, Keith, a bowling ball salesman, and Fred, a long-distance trucker who had to go home in a cab. We had a nice time, really, and Mai Li even made me a little snack at Happy Hour.

The more time I spent with Mai Li, the more I liked her. Who was this nasty old guy trying to take her jewels away, anyhow? I mean really, if all my old boyfriends tried to get their presents back, I'd have to go to work in a towel.

And another thing...Mai Li wasn't so hot at English. I couldn't imagine her putting up much of a defense against the sleazy attorney who hired me. What if she was an illegal alien? Maybe she had no choice but to split or face deportation. Besides, she wasn't even a hooker anymore. Keith and Fred seemed to like her, and they were regulars.

The more I looked at her baubles, the more I figured they were too big to be real. And the more I thought about the Cadillac, the bigger that dent got.

You're probably wondering what I did about all this. Whether I turned in Mai Li, or went back north empty-handed.

Well, I'm not going to tell you.

County Offices:

Aside from various phone calls and side trips, most of your information will be gathered from the offices located in the courthouse of the county where your scoundrel resides. The most effective way to search for assets is in person. If that is not possible, do the best you can by phone or mail.

ASSESSOR'S OFFICE

The assessor's office contains area maps, a list of county property owners, and the assessed value of all parcels of real property located in the county. It is indexed in the following ways.

ALPHA INDEX: The Alpha Index lists all real property owned by an individual, partners or a company. It is indexed alphabetically by name. Some indexes list residential and commercial property separately, so ask the clerk.

Also, be sure and check for property under any

possible business names, as well as under the names of the scoundrel's spouse and kids. Any name listed on your judgment is fair game. However, if you have a judgment against a man and not his wife, and the property is listed in her name, then you are out of luck.

SITUS INDEX: The Situs Index is a listing of information indexed by property address. First, check out the address in which the scoundrel lives to determine the owner of the property. Is it listed under an unrelated name, and therefore most probably rented by your debtor? Is it owned by the spouse, parents or kids?

Write down any information you can find on the worksheets located at the back of the book. This will allow you to put together a profile of your subject. If he rents, you now have the name and address of his landlord. Landlords usually have a lot of pertinent information about their tenants.

Stuff like...

1.   If the scoundrel still lives there.
2.   If he has moved, where he went.
3.   His work address and phone.
4.   Whether he pays his rent by cash or check, and what bank the check is drawn on.

Whether the landlord shares this information with you is anybody's guess. Usually, they are very protective of their tenants as long as they are good tenants. Then, when the scoundrel burns the landlord, he's more than willing to cooperate with you. Unfortunately, by this time the scoundrel has changed banks, moved, lost his job and left no forwarding address.

113

The Situs Index will also list neighbors who can contribute or confirm the same kind of information. With a good scam, or a great true story, which you've probably got, they could be helpful.

ASSESSOR'S PARCEL NUMBER: This is an index that lists property by the assessor's parcel number. In this index you will find the assessed value of the property.

Within these three indexes you will find...

HOMEOWNER'S EXEMPTION: If a homeowner's exemption is declared, then the owner is supposed to be living on the property.

PARCEL NUMBER: This is used to look up the property on the assessor's map. It is also used to identify the property.

RECORDER'S NUMBER AND DATE: This number indicates the last transaction recorded in reference to the property.

NET ASSESSMENT: The amount that the owner is being taxed on. These numbers are not the real assessed value of the property, but the amount it was valued at the time the property was acquired, plus an added percentage each year. The numbers are usually quite low, but usually is the property worth more than the listed value.

SITUS INDEX: The actual street address of the property.

114

MAILING ADDRESS: Where the tax bills are sent.

USE: Ask the assessor for the translation. Is it a vacant lot, a single family dwelling, a duplex, condominiums or a shopping center?

UNITS: How many units are on the site?

RECORDER'S OFFICE

Property Transfers

GRANTOR/GRANTEE INDEX:

This is a listing of all documents kept by the Recorder pertaining to the transfer of land; Deeds, Grants, Mechanic's Liens, Tax Liens, Claims, Mortgages, Power of Attorneys, Judgments, Trustee's Sales, Notices of Impending Doom.

This index and it's corresponding documents are a wealth of information. It's at its best when it is combined on a microfiche every ten years or more with an update and at its worst when the Recorder has separated the Grantee from the Grantor, and listed each year separately. How the index is compiled can result in whether you spend five minutes looking through ten years of land records, or a couple of hours.

Only you can decide how far back to go. Start with the most recent listings and work back. If your scoundrel is in the habit of giving recorded loans on real estate (called Mortgages, or Deed of Trust/Assignment of Rents) I'd go back thirty years, which is the possible span of a loan. If he's lucky to own a trailer in an RV park, I wouldn't bother.

The Grantor/Grantee Index is a list of property transfers.

115

The GRANTOR grants real property to another.

He is...

> The Seller of a Property
> The Borrower of Money
> The Lessor of a Lease Agreement
> The Defendant on a Judgment
> The Deceased in a Probate
> The Mortgager of a Property (He mortgages the property to another as security on a loan.)

The GRANTEE is the person to whom the property is granted.

He is...

> The Buyer of a Property
> The Lender of Money
> The Lessee of a Lease Agreement
> The Plaintiff on a Judgment
> The Recipient of a Probate
> The Mortgagee or Lien Holder (The one who loans the money, and to whom a mortgage is given.)

Let's try a simple real estate transaction...

Maddie Bunshee sells some Florida swamp land to some poor schmuck from Minnesota. Maddie gets cash, and Howie Crenshaw, the schmuck, gets the deed, mosquito bites and a good shot at an ulcer. Maddie has granted her interest in the property to Howie. Therefore, she is the GRANTOR and Howie is the GRANTEE.

Got it?

Not so fast. Howie doesn't have all the money, so he has to borrow from a bank. He takes out a loan and records a DEED OF TRUST on the property in order to secure the loan. The DEED OF TRUST lists Howie as the GRANTOR since Howie is granting an interest in the property to the bank. The bank is, of course, the GRANTEE.

Now Howie is listed as the GRANTEE for the purchase of the property on the DEED document, and the GRANTOR for the loan from the bank on the DEED OF TRUST document.

Still with me?

There is, of course, a slight complication. The bank won't loan Howie enough money to please greedy little Maddie. So Maddie agrees to carry a second mortgage from Howie. They draw up a another DEED OF TRUST, or MORTGAGE. On it, Howie, the buyer grants an interest on the property back to Maddie, the seller. Howie is now the GRANTOR and Maddie is the GRANTEE on the DEED OF TRUST document.

Aren't you glad we've cleared that up?

Here is a list of documents, their abbreviations, and definitions...

MTG or CONSTR TR D: (Mortgage or Construction Trust Deed) Places a lien on a property in order to secure a loan.

ASGT TR D: (Assignment Trust Deed) Transfers the beneficial interest in a trust deed. Lender sells his interest to a new party.

SUBON TR D: (Subordinate Trust Deed) Lender consents to have his loan become second in priority to a new loan.

117

ASSUMP TR D: (Assumed Trust Deed) Remaining loan amount on a trust deed is assumed by a new borrower under the terms of the original trust deed.

NT DFLT: (Notice of Default) Notice that the terms of a trust deed are in default by the borrower.

CNC NT OF DFLT: (Cancellation of the Notice of Default) Notice that the terms of the loan have been met, and that the borrower is no longer in default. The notice of default is cancelled.

AGM CONVEY: (Agreement of Conveyance) The property owner agrees to convey title of the property to a particular buyer after the terms of a contract have been met.

TERM JT TEN or DECOTH: (Termination of Joint Tenancy) States that the joint tenant is deceased and releases his or her interest in the property to the remaining joint tenant or tenants.

QUIT CLAIM: One party relinquishes his or her claim in a property to another.

DEC DISTR: (Deceased Distribution) Court order assigning the estate of a deceased party to the heirs.

LIEN: A lien places a cloud on the title and may result in an attachment to any and all property owned by that person.

MECN LIEN: (Mechanic's Lien) A lien against the property resulting from non-payment of construction work. It must be paid before the property can be sold.

TAX LIEN: A lien by the state or federal government against an individual.

JUDGMENT: A court placed lien stating the debtor is under obligation to the creditor.

ABSTRACT JUDGMENT: A court ordered lien placed against an individual. No real property by the debtor can be sold in the county of the abstract judgment without the amount of the judgment being satisfied.

RELEASE: Releases the person from the lien.

FS: (Financial Statement) Loan secured by personal property.

FSC: (Financial Statement of a Corporation) Loan secured by a corporation.

FST: Loan secured by uncut timber.

FSF: Loan secured by fixtures.

FS CONT: Continuation of a loan.

FS PTL REL: Financial Statement, Partial Release.

FS TERM: Termination of a loan secured by a financial statement.

NT COMPL: (Notice of Completion) Notice by a property owner that a project has been completed.

HMSTD: (Homestead) Declaration by a property owner that a homestead has been created to protect the property interest.

119

ABON HMSTD: (Abandonment of Homestead) Cancels a homestead.

PWR ATTY: (Power of Attorney) One person designates another as his or her attorney-in-fact to act in his behalf according to the provisions of the document.

REVOK PWR ATTY: (Revoke Power of Attorney) Cancels previously appointed authority.

In all of these documents, the GRANTOR is the person taking the action, and the GRANTEE is the beneficiary of the action.

STATE INDEX OF VITAL STATISTICS:

You do not need to contact the state capital in order to check for birth, death and marriage certificates. This index is available in the Recorder's Office for a span of years, differing from state to state. Before and after the frame of time covered by the index, you must check the county records or through the Vital Statistics Office of your state.

The actual documents listed in the index are kept in the County Recorder's Office where the document was recorded. The index will, however, give you a lot of helpful information, including the county of the event, the date, and the number of the document. It will also tell you the bride's maiden name and both their ages at the time of the wedding.

COUNTY INDEX OF VITAL STATISTICS & THEIR CORRESPONDING DOCUMENTS

The county index lists all marriages, deaths and births, from day one to the present. Some court clerks will require that you buy the document in order to view it (usually about $7.) Others will allow you just to look and copy down the information.

MARRIAGE LICENSE:
    Full name of the groom
    Full maiden name of the bride
    Both birth dates
    Previous marriages for both
    When their previous marriage ended
    Their addresses at the time of the marriage
    Their occupations.
    Education levels.
    Father's name, Mother's maiden name of both the bride and groom.
    Signatures of bride and groom.
    Witnesses.
    Who performed the ceremony and where.

DEATH CERTIFICATE
    Full name of the deceased
    Date of death
    Sex
    Race
    Birthplace
    Date of birth
    Parents

Social security number
Occupation and employer
Place and manner of death
Usual residence
Where buried

BIRTH CERTIFICATE
Full name of child
Sex
Date and place of birth
Parents' names
Race

VOTER'S REGISTRATION

The Voter's Registration of Elections Department can be located in the county buildings or in another building altogether. The registration card is current as of the last election.

> Name, Date of Registration, Marital Status, Address, Birthdate, Birthplace, Political Party, Occupation, Telephone, Signature

SUPERIOR COURT
COUNTY CLERK'S OFFICE

PLAINTIFF'S AND DEFENDANT'S INDEX

This index and its corresponding files contain all Superior Court actions filed in the county.

First glance at the index will tell you if your scoundrel is a habitual offender. If he is the defendant in a number of cases, he's probably as adept at protecting his money after a law suit as he was in getting it from you in the first place.

The files contain a lot of the answers you will need in order to collect your money. Was he served at home or at work? Where is home? Where is work? What time was he served, and what time was the process server unable to locate him at that address? What other fictitious business names is he using? And, who are the plaintiffs in these court actions? Wouldn't it be fun to call them up and schmooze about your mutual scoundrel?

The most useful of all these cases are the divorce actions. Community property is a wonderful thing, it can make an ex-wife sing like a canary. If the action is recent it could be the most complete list that you'll ever find of a man's worth. In fact, I like to think of an ex-wife as a spy in the house of love.

Look for: Full & Maiden Names, Social Security Numbers, Childrens Names & Ages, All Real Property Owned, Tax Records, Businesses Owned, Employers & Salaries, Debt Information, Child Support Payments, Relative's Names, Dates of Marriage & Separation

FICTITIOUS BUSINESS NAME

The Fictitious Business Name Index contains listings of all businesses registered with the county. It is usually indexed both by business name and by owner's name. It will tell you other businesses owned by your subject, and whether the business is a sole ownership. It will also give you the location of the business.

PROBATE INDEX

This is a listing of any wills that have made their way into probate. It is sometimes listed in the Plaintiff's and Defendant's Index and sometimes in its own index.

CRIMINAL INDEX

This is a list of any felony charges against the subject. The state vs..... If the case is still pending, the file is usually available for public viewing. It should contain all personal information, including a mug shot. It will also probably contain the name of the bail bondsman, whom I have found to be quite helpful in sharing information. They usually have an entire credit application, as well as current information on the subject.

MUNICIPAL COURT
COUNTY CLERK'S OFFICE

Although these records originate at a city wide level, you do not usually need to go to each municipal hall in order to view them. They are kept at the county offices as well.

CIVIL INDEX: This contains the same sort of records as you will find on the superior level, except they deal with lower court matters. Eviction notices are filed here.

SMALL CLAIMS INDEX: These could be filed separately or in the civil index. They are lawsuits filed under a certain dollar amount.

CRIMINAL INDEX: These are misdemeanor charges, including drunk driving.

TRAFFIC: This is an index of any traffic tickets received in the county. It is a very good source of current information, as the recipient has very little control over being listed in the index.

Lots of information is listed on the microfiche or in the computer. Even more of it is on the ticket itself. Ask to see it.

Look for...
> Full name
> Date of birth
> Current address
> Physical description
> Time, date and location of the violation
> Plate number
> Registered owner of the car
> Year, make, model and color of the car.
> Work address (sometimes)

TAX COLLECTOR'S OFFICE

SECURED TAX ROLLS: For real property. These are usually identical to the index found in the Assessor's Office.

UNSECURED TAX ROLLS: These are the tax rolls of personal property, such as a business.

FISHING AND HUNTING LICENSES: These reveal the full name, date of birth and address of the subject.

PET LICENSES: These may or may not be listed under the owner's name. If so, they will contain the owner's name and address.

BUILDING & PLANNING DEPARTMENTS

If someone is building a new structure or adding onto an existing one, the plans will be filed in the Building Department. If any zone or variance applications are required, they will be listed with the Planning Department as well.

In the Building Department, you can sometimes actually get a floor plan of the house. Of course, some people might consider this none of your business, but I figure if the law has made the information available to the public, then they have made the moral decision for you. This kind of information is valuable in determining the value of the structure, as well as a clue to the personal property that might be located within the house.

The Building Department is also an excellent source of business income information if you are investigating a contractor. Normally, you have to have the address of the structure in order to access the file. In smaller offices, however, the clerks know right off the top of their heads which contractors are working on which houses.

City Offices:

BUSINESS LICENSES

Most cities license certain types of companies that operate within the city limits. Restaurants and shops, for example.

BUILDING PERMITS

These are the same sort of items that are found on the county level, except these list building permit applications that pertain to construction within the city limits.

State Offices:

MOTOR VEHICLE DEPARTMENT

Motor vehicle registration and information on drivers can be obtained either by visiting your local DMV office or by writing to the state office. The state indexes information in three ways...

ALPHA SEARCH: The complete name and locale of the subject is run in order to determine the vehicles and boats registered to that person.

FULL NAME, DRIVER'S LICENSE #, OR BIRTH DATE: This will show an address, the driving record, physical description and the license plate of the car being driven when the ticket was issued.

127

LICENSE PLATE NUMBER: If no cars are registered to your subject, you might want to run the plate of the car he drives. This will tell you what name, or company name, the car is registered under. It might reveal a clue as to another business name, or under whose name he is hiding assets. Running the plate will also reveal the legal owner of the car.

DEPT OF CONSUMER AFFAIRS

This state agency licenses and regulates the following businesses and professions.

Accountants
Advertising
Appliances
Athletic Clubs
Auto Repair Shops
Banks
Beauty Salons
Cemeteries
Collection Agencies
Contractors
Cosmetics
Cosmetologists
Dance Studios
Dentists
Doctors
Dry Cleaners
Employment Agencies
Engineers
Funeral Directors
Embalmers

Geologists
Health Professions
Health Studios
Insurance
Home Furnishings
Home Improvement
Investments
Landscape Artists
Marriage Counselors
Nurses
Nursing Homes
Optometrists
Physicians
Private Investigators
Real Estate Brokers
Repair Services
Repossessors
Service Stations
Utility Companies
Veterinarians

You can contact them by phone or mail. The information is in the state government section of your phone book. Expect to find the full name of the owner of the business, company name, licensing status, address of the business, date of birth of the owner, sometimes social security number, and other pertinent information.

DEPARTMENT OF JUSTICE

The Registry of Charitable Trusts is listed in this office, and it is a list of all nonprofit organizations that are soliciting funds in the state. All nonprofits, aside from churches, must submit their income tax returns to be eligible and all records are public access.

DEPARTMENT OF REAL ESTATE

Regulates all brokers and sales people operating in the state.

SECRETARY OF STATE

CORPORATE STATUS DIVISION: This division keeps records of all corporations registered in the state. If you can supply them with a corporate name, they will give you the corporate status, and the name and addresses of the officers, including the agent of service. In some states, corporations may be listed also by owner's name.

LIMITED PARTNERSHIPS: This division contains the same sort of records as the Corporate Status Division, but for limited partnerships.

NOTARY PUBLIC: Official documents are usually notarized, and you can track down the notary public who signed the document by providing this office with the number on the stamp. This is useful in finding other documents that were signed that same day by the same parties, but were not publicly recorded.

UNIFORM COMMERCIAL CODE: Just as a lien is placed on real property through a deed of trust or mortgage, business property or anything other than real property can be tagged has having a interest by a third party. If someone leased-to-own a photocopy machine, for example, it would fall in this category. Very useful in determining a social security number, and business assets.

ALCOHOL CONTROL BOARD

This agency licenses and regulates any business that sells liquor to the public. This includes restaurants, bars, caterers, liquor stores and wholesalers. The information is usually available by phone.

CONTRACTORS LICENSING BOARD

This agency keeps records of licensed contractors in your area. Names, addresses, complaints, etc.

You the listing under state government in the phone book, but most states have local district offices.

STATE BOARD OF EQUALIZATION

Anyone who sells goods on a retail basis is eligible to purchase those goods without paying sales tax, as long as they charge sales tax when they resell them. The application for the RESALE LICENSE is public access, and it contains the following information...

Business name and address
Owner's name and address
Type of business
Starting date of business
Resale permit number

Federal Offices:

MILITARY RECORDS

To locate someone on active duty, supply the office with the person's full name, social security number, and date of birth. The fees differs, so send along a blank check marked, *"Not to exceed $10.00.""*

U.S. AIR FORCE: Air Force Military Personnel Center, Attn: Worldwide Locator, Randolph AFB, San Antonio, TX 78150.

131

U.S. ARMY: Worldwide Locator Service, U.S. Army Personnel Service Support Center, Fort Benjamin Harrison, IN 46249.

U.S. COAST GUARD: Commandant G-PIM-2, USCG Locator, 2100 2nd Street S.W., Washington D.C. 20593

U.S. MARINE CORPS: Commandant of the Marine Corps, Headquarters, Attn: Locator Service, Washington D.C. 20380.

U.S. NAVY: Navy Locator Service, NMPC No 216, Washington D.C. 20370.

NATIONAL PERSONNEL RECORDS CENTER: To obtain records for retired or discharged military personnel (from all branches of the service). You must enclose a subpoena from a district judge. There is no fee for this service.

They will only supply you with the information you ask for, so ask for...

Marital status
Dependents (name, sex, age)
Last rank and salary
Present, past and future duties
Office phone number
Education level and schooling
Decorations and awards
Photograph
Court martial trials
Social security number
Serial or service number

For deceased persons, ask for...

Dates of service
Date and place of birth
Date, and place of death and burial

VETERANS ADMINISTRATION: This office will not supply a person's address, but they will forward a letter. You must leave the letter in an unsealed envelope so they can check it for threatening messages. Here is the address. Veterans Administration, 536 S. Clark Street, Chicago, IL 60680.

NATIONAL DRIVER REGISTER

The NDRS keeps tabs on drivers who have had a license suspended or revoked and have reapplied in another state. Write them at the National Driver Register Service, Bureau of Public Records, U.S. Dept. of Commerce, 1717 H Street, Washington D.C.

SOCIAL SECURITY OFFICE

These good folks really know how to keep their traps shut. The most they will do for you is to forward a letter to your scoundrel's new address, and then only in the case of an extreme emergency, like a death in the family. If you want to try it, go ahead, but don't tell them I sent you. Write to them at the Office of Public Inquiries, 4100 Annex Building, Social Security Administration, 6401 Security Blvd, Baltimore, MD 21235 (800) 234-5772

133

U.S. DISTRICT
BANKRUPTCY COURT

If your scoundrel has declared bankruptcy, he will be listed in one of several district courts in your state. If your scoundrel goes belly-up and you are named in the bankruptcy, there's not a gosh-darn thing you can do about it. However, if you weren't named for some reason, then the debt still stands.

If you do get a notice of a bankruptcy, check it out! An old scoundrel's trick from way back is to apply for bankruptcy even though the scoundrel knows he is not eligible. (He may have already declared bankruptcy in the last seven years.) Sometimes, before eligibility is determined, the forms are sent out to all the creditors announcing the bankruptcy. When it is denied, the creditors are never notified of the denial. They are left with the impression that the bankruptcy went through. What a nice coup for the scoundrel!

U.S. POSTAL SERVICE

Post office box applications are public access, when the box is being used to solicit business. You can ask for the name of the box holder, address and phone number. If the box is for personal use, you can obtain information from the application only with a court ordered subpoena.

Local post offices keep forwarding addresses for one year. They can be obtained either in person, at the local post office where your scoundrel resides, or by writing to the Postmaster of that office. Enclose one dollar, and state that you are requesting the information as per the Freedom of Information Act.

134

Other Sources:

LIBRARY

Law libraries and public libraries both stock many useful publications including directories, business indexes and trade magazines. Not all will be pertinent to your subject, but if they are, they can be a wealth of information.

There are many more resources and directories in the library than I could ever hope to list, but here are a few of the more generic ones. If you don't see what you need, ask the librarian. They love it.

TELEPHONE DIRECTORIES: Major libraries will have a complete section devoted to city telephone directories. Most libraries will have local community directories dating back a number of years. These are helpful in determining how long your subject has resided in the area, as well as for finding former spouses, or other names he or she may have used in the past.

CRISS-CROSS & OTHER REVERSE DIRECTORIES: These directories list each address in the district, the occupant and their telephone number. There is also a section which lists telephone numbers, in numerical order, and the corresponding name and address.

Although, directories cannot list unlisted telephone numbers, it is still a most helpful guide. If nothing else, it is the closest you can get to visualizing the neighborhood without visiting it in person. At a glance you can tell if the address is a mail drop, a shopping center, a commercial building, an apartment or a condo. The Polk Directory also sometimes lists an occupation for the occupant. Directories are updated on a yearly basis.

NATIONAL DIRECTORY OF ADDRESSES AND TELEPHONE NUMBERS: This source lists major corporations, associations, state and federal government offices and toll-free numbers.

U.S. GOVERNMENT PRINTING OFFICE DIRECTORY: A directory of all members of the federal government.

GUIDE TO THE CORPORATE EXECUTIVES AND DIRECTORS: This is a guide to corporate executives and their directors. (What can I say? It was well named.)

NEWSPAPER FILES: Major libraries will have an index of several national newspapers as well as one or two local ones. Run your scoundrel's name and company through the index to see if he has had any publicity, good or bad. If the library does not have an index of the local newspaper, you can go directly to the newspaper office itself. The advertising department might even be able to tell you if any advertisements were placed by the business you are investigating.

OCCUPATIONAL DIRECTORIES: Professions licensed by the state are sometimes listed in directories. These include every profession from travel agencies to private investigators. There is also a listing of associations for these professions.

WHO'S WHO: The *Who's Who* series includes *Who's Who in America, Who's Who in Finance and Industry,* and *Who's Who in the West.* These books list anybody who-is or who-is-not a Who in about every category you can think of.

The biographies are compiled by publishers, and employers, and a lot of other people who get a real hoot out of being in Who's Who.

STANDARD & POOR'S CORPORATION RECORDS: This volume includes daily news gatherings on capitalization, corporate background, bond subscriptions, stock data, earnings and financial accounting.

DUN AND BRADSTREET: This the TRW and CBI of the business world. Dun and Bradstreet rates anyone that their subscribers request a rating on.   This includes credit checks on even the smallest of businesses. The information is gathered by checking with banks and other references, as well as visiting the site in person.

Dun and Bradstreet also prints a directory called *The Reference Book of Corporate Management.* It lists the names, financial data and credit ratings of U.S. manufacturers, wholesalers and retailers. *The Million Dollar Directory* lists information on American businesses with a net worth of $500,000 or more. (It's official. A million dollars is now worth just $500,000.) Who Owns Whom lists subsidiaries and associate companies as well as parent companies.

THOMAS REGISTER OF AMERICAN MANUFACTURERS: Sixteen volumes of data on U.S. manufacturers.

UNIWORLD: A directory of American firms operating in foreign countries.

CREDIT REPORTING AGENCIES

Credit reporting agencies such as TRW and CBI are perhaps the most overrated sources of information around. You might, in fact, be eligible to obtain this information, but it would hardly be worth the bother.

To begin with, the information is hardly ever an accurate portrayal of someone's credit history. Both companies collect information only from companies who subscribe to their service. Most companies, department stores, credit cards and the like subscribe to either CBI or TRW. Therefore, in order to get an accurate credit report you should get both. As you will then see, the two reports will look like they have been done on two different people!

In addition, some agencies who subscribe, only extract information from the service. They do not add anything, since it takes time to do so, and does not benefit them in any way. (It only benefits the other subscribers.)

I was once turned down for credit at a national computer store chain. At the time I was a homeowner, my car was paid for in full, I had been paying two mortgages for over four years with never a late payment, and I had every department store credit card known to man. Needless to say, I was a bit chagrined.

I ordered my credit report. Neither of my two mortgage payments was mentioned. I was listed as self-employed, which was true, but self-employment is considered a real black mark to credit companies. (A secretary in a small business actually rates higher points than the owner of the business!)

My four years' worth of car payments went unreported, because my credit union did not subscribe to the service. All my department store credit cards were listed, but because I hadn't used any of them in years, each account balance was zero. It was as if I didn't have them at all.

It was easy to see that I was turned down for credit, not because my credit was bad, but because the companies that I had established credit with did not subscribe to the service!

Aside from this kind of major snafu, the best reason for not bothering to get a credit report, is that it won't tell you what you want to know anyway. It is a list of what someone owes, not where his money is!

True, a percentage of people have a checking account at the same bank where they obtained their Visa or MasterCard. But not all, and usually not scoundrels. Scoundrels change bank accounts like the rest of us change socks. Daily. Or at least weekly.

All in all, the information you might get from a credit reporting agency is not worth doing time for the laws you would have to break in order to get the data in the first place.

SOCIAL SECURITY NUMBER

The social security number will tell you the state in which it was issued. The information could be a clue as to your scoundrel's home state, and perhaps even provide a link to property or assets that he might have stashed there.

The following list could also provide you with some dandy cocktail conversation. Memorize it, and then ask someone for the first three digits of their Social Security number. Then impress them by telling them the state where they lived when they were thirteen. I've been the hit of some very dull parties with this one.

001-003	New Hampshire	433-439	Louisiana
004-007	Maine	440-448	Oklahoma
008-009	Vermont	449-467	Texas
010-034	Massachusetts	468-477	Minnesota
035-039	Rhode Island	478-485	Iowa
040-049	Connecticut	486-500	Missouri
050-134	New York	501-502	No. Dakota
135-158	New Jersey	503-504	So. Dakota
159-211	Pennsylvania	505-508	Nebraska
212-220	Maryland	509-515	Kansas
221-222	Delaware	516-517	Montana
223-231	Virginia	518-519	Idaho
232-236	West Virginia	520	Wyoming
237-246	North Carolina	521-524	Colorado
247-251	South Carolina	525	New Mexico
252-260	Georgia	526-527	Arizona
261-267	Florida	528-529	Utah
268-302	Ohio	530	Nevada
303-317	Indiana	531-539	Washington
318-361	Illinois	540-544	Oregon
362-386	Michigan	545-573	California
387-399	Wisconsin	574	Alaska
400-415	Tennessee	575-576	Hawaii
416-424	Alabama	577-579	D.C.
425-432	Arkansas	580	Virgin Islands
		581-584	Puerto Rico

FOR ROCKFORD WANNABES

Once you have gathered as much information as you can by beating the bushes, you might want to go in for the kill. All of the sources of information listed so far are a matter of public record. All of it can be found out anonymously, without anybody finding out that you found out. But if you want to take a chance, have a little fun, and really get the goods, then go hunting at the local level.

Here is where you might consider some of the legalities. Up until this point you have just been checking documents which have public access. Anyone can do this. Anyone can also go scoundrel hunting as long as it is for their own case. Should you, however decide to do it for other people, and charge them for this information, it is called "acting as a private investigator without a license."

The Department of Consumer Affairs takes a very dim view of this. I know, because this is how I got started in the business.

In any case, I don't suggest you go out hoofing it until you have learned all that you can from your public access sources. When you have this information at your fingertips, then you will instantly know if you are being told the truth or not.

There are four types of folks you'll meet out there in "the field."

THOSE WHO KNOW AND WON'T TELL: These can be landlords who are protective of their tenants' privacy or friends or fellow scoundrels who have a pretty good idea of who you are and why you are there. You just never know. By doing your homework, you should be able to recognize who it is that opens the door.

THOSE WHO KNOW AND WILL TELL: Most of these people are decent upstanding type neighbors with a nose for news.

THOSE WHO DON'T KNOW: People so wrapped up in their own lives that they fail to notice what their neighbors do in the privacy of their own homes.

THOSE WHO LIE: In about a quarter of the location cases that I get, I find the scoundrel right at the "last known address" that I got from the client. The scuzball merely answered the door himself, and announced to the process server that he, the scuzball, had moved.

141

So, you can see now why it is so important to know the answers before you ask the questions. The key to getting all of this information is figuring out who knows what, and who they would be most likely to tell.

A landlord, for example, might not tell a bill collector where his tenant works, but he would tell a delivery person who showed up with a giant melting Easter bunny.

Here is a list of people who might be in the know...

Neighbors, Spouse, Old Landlord, Present Landlord, Little Children, Former Boss, Current Boss, Friends, Enemies, Relatives, Ex-Spouses, Maids, Attorney, Former Attorney, Corner Grocer, Corner Bar Owner, Corner Bookie

THE BEST KEPT
SECRET IN THE BUSINESS

Yes. It's true. A huge source of information that many private investigators swear by are the treasures that they find in your day-to-day trash. (Most p.i.s prefer the term 'trash' to 'garbage'. In fact, most p.i.s prefer trash to garbage.)

Someday it may come out that Charlie's Angels all went through the garbage during the station breaks. I doubt it. I rarely look that good after a day in the dumpster. The only thing I ever found out via the garbage was that my scoundrel was on a banana diet. But it you are one of those people who think they haven't earned their money until they've suffered, try it.

This, by the way, is not illegal. It's just disgusting. I should say it's not illegal as long as you leave the can. Some people do a variation on this theme and bring back the can. Just don't take the cans from too many scoundrels on one rampage or you might get the cans mixed up. Or perhaps the garbage.

A WORD ABOUT PUBLIC ACCESS; FROM THE GUYS WHO GAVE YOU "JUST SAY 'NO'"

Government officials have been known to become foggy on the public access laws when faced with an inquiry. I once had a knock-down drag-out with a clerk when I asked "to see the state marriage index." She told me the records were not open to the public, and nothing I could say would convince her that she was breaking the law by refusing to let me see the index. Finally she admitted that she could look up the information *for me*, but I hadn't asked that! I'd asked to see the records. If you receive a negative reply when you ask to see a public access record, try asking if they will look up the information for you.

The Scoundrel Beside You

"Deny everything and demand proof."
Scoundrel's Creed

FAMILY SCANDAL

One day a man named Kevin James called me from a place called Iowa. His wife, Shirley, was leaving that day, said Kevin, and coming to Northern California with her Uncle Stanley. Kevin wanted me to meet them at the San Francisco airport and follow them that weekend. He suspected they were up to no good.

I considered the request briefly. Taking the case would break three of my cardinal rules. One, there was no time for Kevin to get a retainer to me before I started. And I don't do credit. Two, the chances of getting the information Kevin wanted was slim to none. And three, I might have to work the weekend.

After explaining all this to Kevin, he still wanted to hire me. He wired me money and gave me a description of Stan and Shirley. He was a short wiry man with a halo of black hair around a shiny bald plate. She was in her late thirties, plump, with brown hair she wore in a bun. A real cute couple. They would be arriving at San Francisco Airport that evening and Stanley was to be attending a mortician's convention in the city. (Apparently a bunch of the guys were getting together to talk about dead stuff.) After a couple of days, the couple would be heading for Stan's apartment in Campbell, a sprawling bedroom community of San Jose.

And what had all of this to do with me? Well, apparently Kevin had it in his head that Uncle Stanley and Niece Shirley were having an affair. I whipped out the old Websters to see if this qualified as incest, and technically, it didn't. It was more like "incest/in-law."

Kevin told me the couple had been close ever since Shirley's father died when she was a little girl. He suspected the relationship, as it stood now, had been going on about a year, but Shirley had visited Stan when she was a teenager, and something might have happened then as well. Shirley's three sisters all had dubious bouts with reality. One committed suicide. Another was in the loony bin. And the third was just plain nuts.

Kevin suspected Uncle Stanley was behind the families' strange history and that he had been sexually abusing Shirley and her sisters since they were children. On what he based these suspicions he didn't say, and it was the sort of thing that was difficult to ask about. There's a fine line to walk when you're a private investigator. On the one hand, you're paid to get the dirt, and on the other hand, you have this natural inclination to respect your client's privacy. What usually happens is you get the dirt some other way, when the client could have just told you at the beginning and saved himself a lot of time and money. But Kevin wasn't ready to air the family secrets.

I passed on the airport scene. I mean think about it. Kevin wanted me to go to San Francisco International Airport, meet flight 842, find and tail a bald man and a brown haired middle aged couple to the baggage claim area, and then follow them as they (1) took a cab, or (2) took an airport bus, or (3) took a shuttle, or (4) retrieved Stanley's car from long term parking. During the time they were accomplishing this, I was to run to my car in the lot in terminal C and catch them at the curb, or as they came out of long term parking. All this was assuming I picked the right bald haired man and brown haired woman. I mean who did this guy think I was, Rockford?

I also passed on Fisherman's Wharf. There he wanted me to see if they checked into the same room and then wait around in the hall all night long to see if they came out. This was assuming, of course, that the hotel had no security, or if they did, they didn't mind people sleeping *outside* the rooms.

Finally Uncle Stan and Shirley made their way to Campbell. I had already checked out the joint - and Stanley as well.

He was a man without a past. The only record of him in the County Courthouse was when he bought his condo - one of many in a cluster of nondescript buildings that looked more like apartments than something a person might actually purchase.

Other than that, Stanley had done nothing to distinguish himself from the rest of humanity. He had no criminal history, something Kevin had been sure of. He had no liens or judgments against him. He paid his taxes on time. He'd bought no other property, had not been married since his divorce ten years before. He had a teenage son who lived with him in the condo, and the kid checked out as well.

Nonetheless, Kevin wanted me to continue. Stan and Shirley had said they would be staying in the condo, but Kevin wanted to know just *where* in the condo Shirley was supposed to be sleeping. Well, how the heck was I supposed to know!

I first cased the condo on a Friday afternoon, and found Stan and Shirley watching TV in Stan's tiny living room. Stan's place was one flight up from street level. An outside staircase wound up to the third floor, passing Stan's balcony. This was one vantage point, but it was totally visible from the sidewalk that ran through the complex. The other choice was to crouch on the cement "roof" that covered the underground-parking area. This roof was right next to Stan's balcony, separated by only a wooden railing, conveniently riddled with knot holes. The roof was also visible from the sidewalk, and littered with kids. Not exactly a good lurking spot.

I hung around a couple of hours and even followed them to dinner, sitting beside them in the waiting area until their table was ready. They talked quietly, but otherwise there was no intimacy. No holding hands, no touching, no nothing. When finally they went to the table, they sat on opposite sides of the booth. There was absolutely nothing to indicate that they were intimate, and resembled a long married couple who were no longer glowing in each other's company. All in all, they looked pretty grim. They ordered no wine, nor anything else that a courting couple might. And the restaurant they'd chosen was anything but romantic. It was a brightly lit family joint with a good looking pizza.

When Shirley left to make a phone call, I followed. I passed her in the small outer room of the ladies' bathroom, and went on in. From just the other side of the door, I listened as she talked long distance with her mother. She'd promised to call at a certain time, and Shirley was a good daughter. She'd stopped her dinner to call her mom and tell her they were still eating and she'd call her back in twenty minutes from Stan's. Shirley asked about Kevin, but didn't want to talk to him. It was obvious from the conversation that Mom was staying with Kevin and watching the kids.

The couple finished and returned promptly to the condo, where Shirley again called Mom, this time from the living room which I had under surveillance from the tiny peep hole in Stan's fence. The glass doors were closed and I could hear none of the conversation, but I could watch all I wanted. Shirley sat at the desk as Stan, head bowed, sat right beside her, solemnly listening. Pretty soon Shirley looked agitated and I gathered she was talking to Kevin. This went on for about an hour and then it was over.

I called Kevin but, of course, he knew more about the conversation that I did because he was actually *talking* to Shirley and I was just looking at her through a tiny peep hole.

During those long tedious hours of surveillance, it was impossible not to think about the case. Was it true? Were Shirley and her Uncle Stanley *doing it?* And with the blessing of Mom? Or was Kevin wrong about the relationship? Was it merely the father-daughter situation Shirley insisted it was? Many times an affair is only in the spouse's head, and no matter how hard they try to prove adultery, they can't because there is nothing to prove. Was this the case?

Finally Kevin sent me something that made up my mind. It was photocopied pages from Shirley's diary, and love letters from "Uncle Stanley."

We're talking downright sickening. Shirley gushed like a teenage girl over her uncle, and wrote, more than once that she couldn't wait to be back "in Uncle Stanley's arms." The dates were recent, dating back to a trip they took together to North Carolina four months prior. There was a love poem from Stan that referred to that time when his "life began." Life began for Stan, apparently on a Sunday morning after brunch. Although not going into graphic detail, if it wasn't referring to intercourse, then they've invented something new I don't know about.

Kevin was sure of the incestuous relationship and, for the first time, I agreed. In the event of divorce, he did not want his children raised by Shirley and Stan, and that was the reason for the investigation.

But, ironically, the reason I agreed had nothing to do with what I'd observed first hand about the couple. They had done nothing to indicate an intimacy of any kind, and if called to testify in court, I would have to admit that. I told Kevin to bury this investigation, because it would do more to prove his wife's propriety than to help him in an adultery case. The question I put to Kevin was, why hire me? Didn't he see he had more on his wife than I could ever get? After all, he was free to go through her things, read her mail, check her phone bill, and listen in on her telephone conversations. All I could do was follow from a distance and peep through knot holes. Take that diary to the judge, I advised Kevin, and the kids are yours.

The case wasn't officially over until I was chased out of the parking lot by a "neighborhood watch committee" of three eleven-year-old boys on bicycles.

Not my finest hour.

THE TWO KINDS OF CLIENTS

There are only two kinds of clients when it comes to adultery cases. The clients who are right. And the clients who are wrong.

THE CLIENTS WHO ARE WRONG

The clients who are wrong are the hardest to satisfy. These are the people who always have and always will think someone is cheating on them. They thought it about their first marriage, and that marriage failed. The wife said it failed because of her husband's womanizing, and he said it failed because of her suspicious nature. (I suppose, technically, if he was a womanizer and she wasn't suspicious, then there wouldn't have been a problem, right?)

So, if you think your spouse might be cheating on you, ask yourself this; Do you have a history of good and trustful relationships, or have you always been the victim of a cheating lover? If it's the latter, then consider that perhaps you're the sort of person who will never *really* trust anyone. Yes, it could be in your head.

Another thing to think about...

If you are wrong, what will you accept as proof? Remember, given enough time and money, you have a shot at proving adultery. But you can never prove *fidelity*. If you hire someone to follow your husband and he behaves himself for one evening, can you accept your marriage is solid? (Cost, at $50 per hour - $200 to $300) If he's good as gold for ten hours a day for a week? (Cost, $3,500) For a month? ($15,000!) Think about it. Even if someone is having a torrid affair, the couple may only get together infrequently. At what point can you say to yourself, "there, now, I

151

feel better. I was wrong. Now I can relax and get on with my life"?

THE KIND WHO ARE RIGHT

People ask me to follow their lovers for one basic reason. They have observed behavior that is suspicious, have usually confronted their partner about it, the person has denied it, and now they want to know the truth. Once my client knows the truth, they feel they can confront the other person, and he or she will either start behaving him or herself or...

Let's start with the "or". If you do this, if you find out *for sure* that your lover is cheating on you, then you can no longer ignore the situation. You must act. You must either give that person an ultimatum - and stick to it - or condone the situation, either quietly, or after a confrontation. If you go the confrontation route - and the cheating doesn't stop - then you have given tacit permission for the affair to continue.

So think about it. Do you *really* want to know? And, more importantly, what will be your plan of action if and when you *do* know? If you are not emotionally ready to break the tie, then wait until you are. In the meantime, watch and wait. Don't worry, I'll tell you what to watch for.

WHY SURVEILLANCE IS
NOT USUALLY THE ANSWER

Well, think about it. People like to do it *inside*, don't they? And anybody you hire for this awful job, will be *outside*? That's an inherent problem.

There are lots of reasons for people to go inside together, and adultery is just one of them. So if going

inside together doesn't cut it in the evidence department, just what does?

Quite frankly, not much. Private eyes who get
a kick out of this kind of thing - and therefore do it
more than I do - have some tricks I'm perfectly willing
to pass along to you. One thing is 'taping the door.'

'Taping the door' isn't really 'taping the door'
anymore, since some hot-shot attorney proved in
court that it was possible to open and close a door and
have a piece of tape snap back into position. Instead,
now match sticks are commonly used.

The idea is to tuck a bent match stick into the
hinged side of the door down low where it won't be
noticed. If your partner goes into a hotel room with
someone of the opposite (or same) sex, and the match
stick is still intact in the morning, then it can be
concluded neither party exited the room during the
night.

Still, it doesn't prove they had sex, does it?

Another thing p.i.s consider is whether the
lights are left on all night long. If the lights are on,
there are lots of things two people can be doing, and
it is almost impossible to convince a court of law that
sex was part of the evening's entertainment.

Lighting, of course, really means nothing. It's
quite possible to have sex with the lights on. It's not
illegal, or even immoral, just a strong jolt of reality that
most people find unpleasant. And it's not unheard of
to leave the lights on in the living area while the romp
happens in the bedroom. This is done usually to
confound the poor p.i. who's snoozing in the stairwell.
So what if you go to all this expense, and your partner
leaves the lights on? You've got nothing, that's what.

Say they show affection in public, is this "proof?"
If by affection you mean searching the floor of your
husband's car for her bobby pin for three hours, it
might not be "proof," but it's highly suspicious.

If by affection you mean going to dinner, holding hands and kissing, then what you have is a spouse who goes to dinner with someone else, holds her hand and kisses her. If you confront him with this "evidence," and he says, yeah it's true, but they didn't do anything else, will you believe it? More importantly, if he says he won't do it anymore, can you believe him?

What all this comes down to is - if your spouse's words and actions don't jive, then he or she is lying to you. They could be, and probably are, lying to cover up an affair, but they may never admit that. At some point - without *absolute proof*, and without a confession - you have to look at the facts and come to an intelligent conclusion.

SO WHAT ARE THESE FACTS?

By the time most people come to me, they know in their hearts their spouse has been lying to them. They have witnessed strange and unusual behavior, and have, most times, confronted their partner about it, and gotten some lame-brained excuse. My client has swallowed it. Or tried to.

But the suspicions haven't gone away, and neither has the erratic behavior. Now they want to know the truth. Are they nuts, as their mate claims, or do they have a legitimate gripe?

I can respect that, but I have to say, in almost every case, they already have all they need before they come to me. Surveillance, as I hope I've shown, costs a whole lot of money, and most times prove nothing.

What with no-fault divorce, is it really important to *prove* infidelity, except for your own justification in doing what you feel you must do anyway? Isn't it enough that your relationship has deteriorated to such a degree that you're miserable?

WHAT YOU CAN DO

What you can do is to gather "evidence" that you can examine independently of your partner's explanations. This whole book is built on the concept of following "paper trails," and as an insider you have access to everything you need.

Think about the paper trails that your partner creates just in living his or her life.

Mileage for example. If your husband says he's driving to Sacramento for a business meeting, and the mileage on his car shows he's only gone as far as the corner grocery, doesn't that *prove* he's lied to you?

What about his credit card receipts? Are there charges for motels you know are just down the street? Are there listings for jewelry stores and flower shops, on dates when you've received no gifts?

How about his checkbook? Bank statements? Has he taken out large amounts of cash from the automated teller machine, and then done the same thing the very next day? What happened to the money?

What about the phone bill? What about his calling credit card? The bill from his car phone? Now, unless all the calls are local, you know exactly who he has been dialing. If the telephone is in your name as well - and it should be - call Ma Bell and check on those charges. If a number appears on your bill, they'll tell you who it is registered to.

What about his income tax returns? Has he declared interest from a savings account you didn't know existed? Has he listed a cabin in the Catskills as a second residence? Has he deducted $500 in sales tax for a boat or a car you know nothing about? Has he listed a safe-deposit box rental as a business expense? What about other business expenses - that $3,000 for travel and entertainment, for example. (If

155

you suspect the income tax returns you're reading are phoney - request an official copy from your closest regional internal revenue office. Ask for Form 4506, a *"Request of Copy for Tax Return."*)

OTHER STUFF

There are other signs, that while they prove nothing, could still spell trouble.

Like, has your partner suddenly started wearing clean (and fancy) underwear? Is he or she more careful in their appearance? Losing weight? Hanging out at the tanning salon? Going overboard in the cosmetic surgery department? Again, by itself, this stuff proves nothing, but there's normally some ritualistic grooming that happens at the beginning of mating season, and you should be aware of it.

NOW WHAT?

Well, now you know. You have "proof" in black and white that you can compare to the version you are getting from your spouse. If they jive, then your fears were unfounded. Whew!

If they don't jive, whether (and when) you go for a confrontation is up to you. But never let go of the facts. And if your partner *never ever* confesses, and the excuses are lame, then at some point you must go with what you *know,* and not what you hear.

Good luck.

Pre-Business Check

"I don't do shootouts."
Rat Dog Dick Company Motto

It is probably too late now or you wouldn't have bought this book in the first place...

But next time, before you enter into a major deal with a potential scoundrel, give the matter an hour or so of your time in the county courthouse.

If he has been in the area for a couple of years, you can get a good indication of his or her business dealings. If he is new in town, either check him out in the county he came from, or tread lightly.

If a San Francisco investment firm had just followed this advice they would have saved their clients from a modern day cattle rustler.

SCOUNDREL ON A ROPE

The Bennington Cattle Company had two business plans. One was a traditional feed-lot setup where cattle breeders would fatten their cows prior to slaughter. The second was to sell investors a number of cattle, leave them on the feed lot to fatten, and then sell the cattle for the investors at a profit. The investors would never actually take possession of the cows.

In both cases, the Bennington Cattle Company planned to cut their costs by feeding the cows a mixture of their own recycled manure. (Yuck!)

Toward the end of his life, Mr. Bennington got in a bit of a cash flow crunch. The Arizona Farm Home Association was coming down hard on him to pay back his five million dollar loan, so Bennington decided to kite a few cows. He sold some San Francisco investors a herd of cattle before he actually got around to buying them.

A year later, when the investors came to visit, he showed them his feed lot just brimming with other people's cows. The investors wanted cows and they got cows. No one asked about brands or seemed to notice that the cattle had someone else's brand already on their rears. And in the end, Bennington never quite got around to buying the cows at all. If the San Francisco investors had checked with the branding office in Phoenix before they did business with Bennington, they would have found that out.

The recycled manure hit the fan just days before Bennington was to appear before the District Attorney. That day he "died" in a helicopter crash in Oklahoma. The body was identified by the contents of his wallet and he was cremated before anyone discovered the absence of cattle.

ANOTHER DAY, ANOTHER SCOUNDREL

The strangest scoundrel I ever met was one I wasn't even looking for. In fact, I had trouble getting rid of her.

When I picked up the phone on the third ring, it sounded like she'd started talking on the first.

Beatrice Tierney babbled on about how the S.P.C.A. had taken her 22 dogs away from her and put them up for adoption. She was manic about getting them back. (You get these kinds of cases when you list yourself as Rat Dog Dick in the phone book.)

Now I figure just because someone is too strange to have human friends doesn't mean they should go around being lonely. This woman, however, could possibly have been too weird for even a pet to love.

She arrived at my office dressed totally in black. Black dress. Black chiffon scarf. Black wig. She even had a kind of gray film over her skin. She continued her babbling in my office, but now she started lining up one hundred dollar bills on my desk as she spoke. A practice I do not, by the way, discourage.

Her story was that the S.P.C.A. had taken away all her pooches and Beatrice wanted to find out where they were so she could sue the people who had them and get the little critters back.

Now, I'm not up on doggy-law, but I do know that if it were a legitimate suit, you'd have to sue the S.P.C.A. and, if you won, they'd have to track down your animals and return them to you. Never do you sue some unsuspecting family who just gave Puff-Puff a home. Basically, it was a case of What's Wrong With This Picture?

Time for a little pre-client investigation.

Now, usually I start my investigations at the county courthouse in the county where the alleged scoundrel resides. But Beatrice Tierney was from Hayward, and I didn't want to waste the time or the bridge toll on this case if I didn't have to. Also, I had a feeling this story had made the papers.

I was right. In the index under her name the headline read, "Many Dogs Found Dead at Hayward Kennel." It seems that the S.P.C.A. was called in after police investigated the private kennel. They found two dead dogs on the front lawn and thirteen more stuffed into fifteen gallon drums out back. There were two dozen animals suffering from malnutrition. Several died, even after they were rescued. This woman was so nuts that she couldn't even see that she was killing them. Like Lenny in *Of Mice and Men*, she only wanted to pet them.

If I had taken this job, I would have never forgiven myself. I also would not have been surprised if the state had yanked my investigator's license.

WHERE TO START

You can put together an amazing profile on someone in just a short time. It will soon become obvious if you should (1) rent to (2) do business with, or even (3) marry the scoundrel of your choice.

Check with...

THE RECORDER'S OFFICE
    GRANTOR/GRANTEE INDEX: Look for abstract judgments, mechanic's liens, trustee's sales.

SUPERIOR COURT CLERK
> PLAINTIFF'S INDEX: Does he sue other people without just cause?
> DEFENDANT'S INDEX: Do other people sue him for just cause?
> CRIMINAL INDEX: Does he carry a rod?
> FICTITIOUS BUSINESS NAME: Is there something he's not telling you?

MUNICIPAL COURT
> INDEX, CIVIL & SMALL CLAIMS: Has he been evicted? Are his checks made of silly putty? Is he a Suer? Or a Sue-ee?
> CRIMINAL INDEX: Does he drive drunk?

If the guy comes up clean and has been in the county awhile, he's probably legit. He could, however, only be legit under the brand new name he's using, you never know. Most people, however, don't bother to change their names no matter how much trouble they're in.

If you do find action by or against him, read the file and consider the claim. Good people sue and get sued nowadays. But if he pulls the same scam over and over, and it's the same one you've been hearing, then do like Nancy and just say no!

In 90% of the cases I get as a private investigator, the whole nasty mess could have been prevented if my client had checked out his opponent before doing business.

WHAT ABOUT THE OTHER 10%?

Usually when you check out a scoundrel, you will find only a small percentage of information on him. You can check thirty sources and be lucky if you find him in five indexes.

This could be for one of two reasons. First, only a small percentage of people who have been suckered by a scoundrel will initiate civil proceedings. Most of a scoundrel's sins will go unreported, either out of a sense of futility or justified embarrassment on the part of the sucker, er, sorry,....victim.

Another reason you may find nothing in the courthouse, is that the scoundrel is new in town.

FOR SALE: NICE BRIDGE. GOOD PRICE.

Just because you're on vacation, doesn't mean the scoundrels are. Once, on holiday, I visited a friend of mine in Boston. I found her embroiled in the aftermath of a very nasty love affair that lasted three weeks and cost her about $3,500.

Barbara met Jeffrey Popkin in Boston's Back Bay district. She was walking a large rubbery grey-hound that she had saved from extinction when it's career at the race track ended. That should tell you something about her heart.

Jeffrey Popkin approached her and asked her directions to the corner grocery. He said he was new in town and made some inquiries about the neighborhood, the best restaurants, where the laundry was, etc. Being Barbara, she went out of her way to be helpful. She even gave him her phone number in case he had any more questions.

He called to ask her to dinner. When he showed up, however, he had a small problem. He had just gotten his new automatic teller machine card, and the nasty machine had eaten his card! Because it was a weekend, he couldn't get any more money until the banks opened on Monday. Could Barbara spring for dinner and he'd pay her back on Monday?

She did, of course, being Barbara and all.

Barbara quickly became Jeffrey's new best friend. After all, he was new in town, all alone in the world, and the first date she'd had in months.

Soon he had even more problems. None of which were his fault. His car got stolen. His ex-wife ruined his credit in the divorce. A cop stopped him for some misunderstanding and his driver's license was yanked. He was stopped again for driving without a license and ended up in the slammer. He couldn't keep their date because he was in a cocaine rehabilitation center until Thursday. (Just visiting, Jeffrey?)

The next week he had yet another problem. Again, he couldn't access cash, it being the weekend and all. Could Barbara get money from her ATM and exchange it for his $500 check?

In the meantime, Jeffrey started his new job as a salesman. The company was to pay for Jeffrey's accommodations until he was settled, so Jeffrey moved out of his boarding house into a hotel. All this happened on a weekend, of course, and again, Jeffrey couldn't access any money. And again, Barbara cashed his $500 check.

There was another problem as well. It seemed he'd neglected to get his company credit card on Friday and the hotel required one for booking purposes. Could Barbara show the hotel her credit card (for identification purposes only, mind you) until Jeffrey was able to get his on Monday?

Oh c'mon, Jeffrey. This is Barbara we're talking about. It's a given!

Soon afterward these money problems began to wear on the couple's idyllic bliss. Jeffrey was late for, sleep-walked through, or didn't bother to show up for more and more dates. Of course he always had a good reason. Once some friends flew him to Atlantic City on the spur of the moment for a little gambling. Another time, he had to go see his ex-wife over some kid thing.

Meanwhile, Barbara went on being Barbara. She made him home cooked meals, for which he never showed up. She bought him a nice Father's Day gift, which he accepted and then returned for cash. She did some other stuff, which is really none of your business, or mine, if you get my drift.

Her first real indication that something was very, very wrong was when the first check came back marked "no such account."

She called him and he replaced it with another check on another bank which came back the following week marked, "no such account."

Being the sensitive soul that she is, Barbara got a little stressed out. She even called him up and pouted. He took great offense at that and hung up on her. She, of course, called back to apologize.

Soon, they could not have a conversation without Barbara bringing up the $1,000 he owed her. Jeffrey, of course, thought this quite rude. He told her that he didn't want money to come between them, and if she was going to talk about money all the time not to bother to call at all. Barbara apologized and sent him a cute little "please forgive me" card.

Soon he didn't call anymore at all. When she called, he wasn't there. When he returned, he never returned her calls. Well, Barbara's no dummy. She could see the handwriting on the wall. It was over! There were some residual feelings, of course. Hurt. Betrayal. Embarrassment. And, oh yes, that bit about the credit card.

She called the hotel. Yes, he was still there. And yes, his expenses were indeed being charged to her credit card.

She called the credit card company. She explained that the credit card was to be used for identification purposes only, so what's going on?

"Did the hotel write that on the charge slip?" the clerk asked. Barbara didn't know. Well, never mind, said the clerk. Write a letter to the hotel, and to the credit card company, stating that the card is to be used for identification purposes only. Send it registered to both.

She did. And made a call to the hotel to confirm it. Just to be safe, she cancelled the credit card.

Six weeks later, she got a phone call from the credit card company. She was $2,500 over her limit! It seems that despite the certified letter to the hotel, they had continued to accept it as payment!

The hotel claimed they routinely, at each $300 increment, called the credit card company to check the limit and authorization of the account. They had done this four times *after* the credit card was cancelled, and received authorization each time.

There was only a $500 credit limit left on Barbara's card when Jeffrey moved into the hotel. Yet, the hotel allowed him to charge $2,000 *over the limit* on a *cancelled* credit card, after they received a letter stating the charges were *fraudulent!*

Makes you want to leave home without it, doesn't it?

SO, WHAT'S YOUR POINT?

My point is, don't go through life being a schmuck. (No offense, Babs.)

I arrived to visit Barbara two days before she received the phone call from the credit card company telling her she owed them for $2,500 worth of charges on her cancelled credit card. We went together to the county courthouse in Boston to check out the elusive Jeffrey Popkin. Yet there was no record of him. It was as if he'd never been born.

But, of course, he wasn't a good guy at all, he just hadn't been in Boston long enough to have his bad deeds recorded on public record.

As of this writing, Jeffrey Popkin is still clean, as far as the courthouse records go. He has left the hotel and made off for parts unknown. Because of that, Jeffrey Popkin is unservable, and therefore unsueable. and, as far as public records go, Jeffrey Popkin is an unknown, and therefore an apparent good guy.

HOW CAN YOU IDENTIFY A SCOUNDREL?

Look for the signs. Scoundrels have certain personality traits, business practices and habits. Now, just because a person does one or more of these things doesn't mean he or she is a scoundrel, but put them together and the odds are, here comes trouble.

1. Scoundrels deal only in cash. For tax purposes, it behooves most of us to handle money transactions by check or credit card. Quite simply, we need the documentation for expense account and tax purposes. Anyone who deals solely in cash, is usually either hiding the money from creditors or the IRS, or is making money in a cash business and not reporting it.

2. They're new in town. Now, new-in-town is my middle name, so I don't like to talk. But people who move around, pull up stakes and arrive in a city, friendless after they hit their thirties are

either very adventuresome, or in a whole peck of trouble someplace else. People who live normal, non-scoundrel-like lives are, unfortunately, too established by thirty to throw it all away on adventure.

3. Trouble is their middle name. Okay, things happen. We all have a tough time of it now and again. But when someone is constantly the victim of...schizophrenic ex-wives, card-eating automatic teller machines, stupid bank errors, money greedy landlords, unreasonable S.W.A.T. teams, etc., etc., etc.,...beware! If you hear the phrase, "It's not my fault," twice in the first week you meet someone, buy a ticket on the first bus to Omaha. And pay for it in cash, so he can't trace you!

4. They make friends easily. Again, I make friends easily. There's nothing wrong with that. But not best friends. If you meet someone and immediately, you're their closest friend, the one they rely on to get them out of jams and to borrow money from, then think twice. People whose best friends are their newest friends are usually bad news.

5. They're secretive. Some people are just private people. You can sit next to them on a five hour flight and never even hear their life story. That's okay. But if you can never get a home or work phone number, then something's wrong. People in trouble avoid paper trails. That's why they deal in cash. That's why the phone is unlisted. That's why their answering machine doesn't state who you've called, or what number you've

167

reached, or when the party will return. Again, none of this is cut and dry. It's just one of the signs.

6. They're misunderstood, at odds with everyone around them. No one understands them. Not their employer. Not their roommate. Not their landlord. And, not one of their six ex-wives. When everyone is mad at someone, usually everyone is right.

7. They pay their rent weekly. Or, even worse, they don't pay it at all (For some entirely justifiable reason, of course.) Anybody who hits adulthood and lives in a rented room or hotel, without roots, without furniture, and without friends, is suspect. It's hard to get to age thirty without acquiring a whole garage full of stuff.

8. They have cash-flow problems, especially on weekends. I never borrow money. Not from my friends. Not even from my parents. If I need cash, I get a cash advance on my credit card and pay it back at 18% interest. People who borrow money from people they've just met are usually TROUBLE.

So there it is. Eight signs of the times in The Age of the Scoundrel. Again, a lot of us possess one or two of these traits. But get involved with someone who possesses three or more of these traits and you'll be qualified to write your own book!

Business Letters

The following are some samples of letters you can send your scoundrel in hopes that he/she will come to his/her senses before you annihilate their credit, careers and personal lives.

NOTICE OF C.O.D.
BAD CHECK LETTER
COLLECTION LETTER
DEMAND FOR PAYMENT
SECOND REQUEST FOR PAYMENT
FINAL NOTICE BEFORE LEGAL ACTION
INSTALLMENT AGREEMENT TO PAY DEBT
AGREEMENT TO COMPROMISE DEBT

NOTICE OF C.O.D.

Date:

To:

Dear:

    Thank you very much for your purchase order dated _____,19___ which we received on _____,19__(copy enclosed).

    At this time we are unable to extend credit for the sale of the merchandise. Therefore, unless you notify us to cancel the order within _____ days of receipt of this notice, we will ship the merchandise C.O.D.

Very truly yours,

_____

BAD CHECK LETTER

Date:

To:

Dear:

This is to inform you that your check dated
_____19__, made payable to_____,
in the amount of $_____, has been returned to
us due to insufficient funds.

We realize that such things do occur and
therefore are bringing this matter to your attention
so you can take the opportunity to correct this error
and issue us a new check.

It is our policy to retain the old check until a
new check has been issued and cleared. If we do
not receive payment in full, we will pursue legal
action to the full extent of the law. We are confident
that you will resolve this matter and look forward to
doing business with you again in the future.

Our thanks for your attention to this matter.

Very truly yours,

_____

COLLECTION LETTER

Date:
Name of CEO:
Address:

Dear Mr_____,

RE: PAST DUE AMOUNT: $_____

     We are now in the process of inventorying those accounts we consider to be seriously past due.

     The decision whether or not to place an account with a collection agency is one we do not make lightly - especially in your case.

     Your goodwill is important to us, and we would like to continue doing business with you for many years to come. Because of this we are reluctant to take any action which might jeopardize your good credit, or cause you embarrassment or added expense. The terms of our agreement, as you may remember, stipulate that you will be responsible for any expense incurred in the collection of your account. This, of course, included legal fees.

     I think you must agree that our position is a fair one. We have extended you credit based on your promise to pay. We have contacted you numerous times without response, and now we must consider placing your account with our collection agents or a law firm.

     Hopefully, it will not come to that. I am personally suspending further action until ____, 19__ in hopes that you will act promptly and forward your check FOR THE FULL AMOUNT to us immediately.

     It is important that you respond by _____. Otherwise, a decision must be made that I am sure neither of us wants.

Very truly yours,

_____

DEMAND FOR PAYMENT

Date:

To:

RE: Obligation dated_____19,__ by and
          between _____and _____

Dear:

You are currently in default of the obligation referred to above. Demand is hereby made of you for full payment of $_____.

Very truly yours,

_____

SECOND REQUEST FOR PAYMENT

Date:

To:

RE: Obligation dated_____19,__ by and
          between _____and _____

Dear:

In our letter dated _____,19__ we informed you that $_____ remained overdue on your account. To date no payment from you has been received. We once again request payment.

Very truly yours,

_____

FINAL NOTICE
BEFORE LEGAL ACTION

Date:

TO:

Re: $_____ PAST DUE

    We have repeatedly requested payment of the
above past due account. Our demands for payment
have been ignored. Therefore, we shall turn this
account over for collection within the next ____ days
unless payment, or an acceptable proposal for
payment is received. Collection action on this obligation may result in additional legal or court costs
to you and may impair your credit rating.

Very truly,

_____

INSTALLMENT AGREEMENT TO PAY DEBT

Date:

To:

RE: Obligation dated_____19,__ by and
        between _____and _____

Dear:

        This letter serves to confirm our agreement
of_____, 19__, in which you acknowledge the
outstanding overdue debt of $_____ to our
company. We agreed that you shall make consecutive weekly payments of $_____ until the debt
is satisfied in full. We further agreed that I would
receive the first payment by _____,19__
and each successive payment every
_____ thereafter.
        I sincerely appreciate your cooperation in
resolving this matter. Finally, would you acknowledge our agreement by signing the enclosed copy of
this letter and returning it to me in the enclosed,
self-addressed envelope.

Very truly yours,

_____

AGREEMENT TO COMPROMISE DEBT

Date:

RE: Obligation dated_____19,__ by and
between _____and _____

The undersigned, Creditor of _____
(Debtor) hereby agrees to compromise the indebt-
edness due the undersigned Creditor on the following terms and conditions:

1. The Creditor and the undersigned agree
that the present debt due is $ _____.

2. Both parties agree that the undersigned
Creditor shall accept the sum of $_____ as
payment in full on said debt and in complete dis-
charge of all monies due, provided the sum herein
shall be promptly paid in the following manner:

3. In the event the Debtor fails to promptly
pay the   compromised amount, the undersigned
Creditor shall have the right to prosecute its claim
for the total debt due under paragraph 1 less any
payments made.

4. This Agreement shall be binding upon and
to the benefit of the parties, their successors and
assigns.

Signed and sealed this____day of _____, 19__.

_____   _____
        Debtor   Creditor

Worksheets

The following worksheets should prove helpful in your asset search.

INITIAL REPORT: List the original information you receive. When you find conflicting info., compare it with the original to see if you are referring to the right guy, or someone else with the same name.

RECORDER'S OFFICE/COUNTY CLERK: Copy off the microfiche any info. you need to look up.

ASSESSOR'S OFFICE: List Real Property info.

REAL PROPERTY: List properties you find in the Assessor's Office, plus those in the Grantor/Grantee Index dated after the Assessor's roll was compiled. Any liens? Has the property been paid for, or lost in foreclosure?

177

MISCELLANEOUS:

FICTITIOUS BUSINESS NAME: List all business names listed in the Owner's Index.

STATE INDEX OF VITAL STATISTICS: List any records of births, deaths or marriages.

POST OFFICE: Check for forwarding address.

PROBATE INDEX: Any relatives who have...left?

DEPARTMENT OF MOTOR VEHICLES: (1) ALPHA INDEX: Registered Vehicles. (2) NAME & DRIVER'S LICENSE: By name and driver's license #, or birthdate for address. (3) PLATE: Run the plate of the car to find the legal and registered owner.

VOTER'S REGISTRATION: For identification and location purposes.

TAX LIENS: For identification and location purposes.

TRAFFIC: For identification and location purposes.

PROFESSIONAL LICENSING BOARD: Business income.

CORPORATE STATUS: For locating business income.

REVERSE DIRECTORY: For location purposes.

ASSET RECAP SHEET: Summarization of assets.

INITIAL   REPORT

INDENTIFICATION

Name (last) _____(first) _____(middle) _____
Social Security # _____ Date of Birth _____
Nickname _____ Driver's Liscense # _____
Address _____

DESCRIPTION

Height _____ Weight _____ Build _____ Eyes _____
Sex _____ Glasses _____ Facial Hair _____

EMPLOYMENT

Occupation _____
Employer_____
Employer's Address_____

VEHICLE

Year_____ Make_____ Model _____
Color _____ Liscense _____

SPOUSE

Name _____
Employer_____
Age _____
Address _____

RECORDER'S   OFFICE
COUNTY   CLERK

(List all documents that you might want to look up.
Then transfer pertinent information to other worksheets.)

Grantor	Doc.#, Date	Grantee	Comments

ASSESSOR'S   OFFICE

Scoundrel ————————— County —————

Date ————

ALPHA INDEX (Look up by name)

Name —————————Situs Address —————
Mailing Address ————— APN# —————————

Business Name ————— Situs Address —————
Mailing Address ————— APN# —————————

SITUS ADDRESS ((Look up by Address)

Address ——————————————————
Owner of Property ————— Address —————
Homeowner's Exemption ———— APN#—————
Assessor's Value ——————————————

ASSESSOR'S   PARCEL   NUMBER (APN#)

APN# ————————— Situs Address —————
Owner —————————Mailing Address —————
Homeowner's Exemption ————Recorder's #————

ASSESSOR'S OFFICE &
RECORDER'S OFFICE

REAL   PROPERTY

PROPERTY (From Assessor's Office, Or from Deed listed
in Recorder's Office after Assessor's Index was compiled.)

Owner's Name ————————————————————
Mailing Address ————————————————————
Situs Address ——————————————————————
Assessor's Value ————————————————————
Land ——————Improvements ——————————
Homeowner's Exemption ———— Zoned Usage ————
Deed Number ——————————Transfer Fee ————

DEED OF TRUST/ASSIGNMENT OF RENTS

Document #———— Beneficiary ——————————
Address ——————————————————————————
Amount ————— Date ——————————————————

REYCONVEYANCE/SATISFACTION OF MORTGAGE

Document #————————————————————————
Date ——————————————————————————————

TRUSTEE'S SALE

Date ——————————————————————————————

MISCELLANEOUS CHECKLIST

VOTER'S REGISTRATION	PROFESSIONAL LICENSING BOARD (State Government)
Name: _____ Address _____ Telephone _____ Date of Birth _____ Occupation _____ Political Party _____ Date _____ Family members _____ listed at same address _____	Name _____ Address _____ Business Name _____ License # _____ Date _____
TAX LIEN (Recorder's Office)	CORPORATE STATUS (Secretary of State)
Name _____ Last address _____ _____ Date _____ Social Security # _____	Corporate Name _____ Address _____ President _____ Vice President _____ Officer of Service _____ Corporate Status _____ Date of Incorporation _____
TRAFFIC	REVERSE DIRECTORY
Name _____ Citation # _____ Date _____ License # _____ Date of Birth _____ Address _____ Type of Car _____ Plate # _____	Address _____ Occupant _____ Neighbors _____

FICTITIOUS BUSINESS NAME (County Clerk's Office) Date_____ Document #_____ Owner's Name_____ Address_____ Name of Business_____ Address_____	**DEPT. MOTOR VEHICLES** ALPHA SEARCH Name_____ Address_____ Vehicle_____ Registered Owner_____ Legal Owner_____ Address_____ Amt. Owed_____ (From legal owner)
STATE INDEX OF VITAL STATISTICS (Recorder's Office) Marriage_____ Birth_____ Death_____ Name_____ Date_____ Document #_____ County_____ Groom_____ Date of Birth_____ Address_____ Occupation_____ Bride_____ Date of Birth_____ Address_____ Occupation_____	**NAME or DR. LICENSE #** (To Locate) Name_____ License #_____ Date of Birth_____ Address_____ Other Address_____ Description_____ PLATE (To Find Legal Owner)_____ Plate #_____ Legal Owner_____ _____ _____
POST OFFICE Name_____ Last Address_____ New Address_____	**PROBATE INDEX** (County Clerk's Office) Date_____ Name_____ Loot_____

ASSET
RECAP LIST
(Use to list all assets worth attaching)

REAL PROPERTY				
Situs	APN#	Value	Liens	Equity

RENTAL INCOME			
Owner	Renter	Address	Rent

PROMISSORY NOTES			
Lender	Borrower	Address	Amount

BUSINESS		
Company	Address	Partners

PLANES, TRAINS & AUTOMOBILES

Legal Owner	Plate #	Balance	Equity

PROBATE & TRUST INCOME

EMPLOYMENT

Employer	Address	Occupation	Salary

BANK ACCOUNTS

Bank & Branch	Address	Account #	$$$$$

Order Of Examination

One tool the court makes available to you is the "Order of Examination." This is a hearing where the two parties meet in court, and you can ask your scoundrel exactly where his money is. He can hardly refuse, as there will be a bench warrant issued for his arrest if he ignores the summons.

This sounds like a much better deal than it usually ends up being. First off, the scoundrel can immediately hide all his assets upon leaving the courtroom. To minimize this risk, I suggest as soon as your scoundrel admits an asset, send someone out to put the writ of attachment into effect. Keep the scoundrel talking, as the legal footwork goes on.

Despite it's drawbacks, I would suggest calling in the debtor for a hearing. You've got nothing to lose, and it makes your scoundrel very nervous, and therefore very unhappy. And after all, isn't that the fun of all this?

187

ORDER OF EXAMINATION

Date of the Examination _____

IDENTITY

Full name _____

Address _____

Work address _____

Home phone _____

Work phone _____

Date of birth _____

Place of birth _____

Spouse's full name _____

Maiden name, or spouse's maiden name _____

OVERVIEW

From where do you receive your primary source of income?

Do you receive any other weekly income? _____

Do you receive any other monthly income? _____

Quarterly? _____

Annual? _____

REAL PROPERTY

PRIMARY RESIDENCE

Do you own or rent the house you live in? _____

Is it owned by your spouse or a relative? _____

Is it an apartment, condominium, town house or house? ____

Who is shown as the owner of the property on the title? ____

Is the property listed in more than one name? _____

If so, what are the names of the other owners? _____

188

What date was the property purchased? _____

For what amount? _____

How much was the downpayment? _____

How much are the monthly payments? _____

How much is currently owed on the property? _____

What is the name of the mortgage company? _____

What is the current market value of the property? _____

LIENS

Is there a second deed of trust on the property? _____

If so, how much is it for? _____

What are the monthly payments? _____

Who do you make the payments to? _____

Are there any other liens on the property? _____

Who do you make these payments to? _____

How much are they for? _____

Who makes the mortgage payments on your home? _____

Are they paid by check, cash or money order? _____

What bank and branch are the checks drawn on? _____

What day of the month are the payments made? _____

RENTAL UNITS

Do you rent out any rooms in your home? _____

How much income do you get from the rents? _____

What is the name of the renter? _____

What is their address? _____

What is their telephone number? _____

Where do they work? _____

When is the rent due? _____

Is it paid by check, cash, or money order? _____

OTHER PROPERTY

Do you or your spouse own any other real property? _____

If so, what is the address of the property? _____

What county and state is that located in? _____

When was the property purchased? _____

By whom? _____

In whose name is the property now held? _____

Is it improved or vacant property? _____

What kind of buildings are on the property? _____

Are they being rented? _____

What are the names and addresses of the renter? _____

What is the monthly rent? _____

When is it due? _____

What is the bank, branch and account number of the bank where
the rents are deposited? _____

Was the property financed? _____

By whom? _____

Address? _____

How much was the down payment? _____

What is the balance due on the property? _____

What are the monthly payments? _____

What is the current market value of the property? _____

IF THE DEBTOR RENTS

Do you have a lease? _____

How much do you pay in rent? _____

Who actually pays the rent? _____

Is it paid by cash, check or money order? _____

What is the name and address of your landlord? _____

Are you up-to-date in your rent payments? _____

What day do you pay your rent? _____

How much is your security deposit? _____

Are the utility bills listed in your name? _____

What name is your telephone listed under? _____

EMPLOYMENT

What is your occupation? _____

Are you currently employed? _____

190

By whom? _____

What is your work address? _____

How long have you worked there? _____

What is your social security number? _____

What is your gross monthly pay? _____

How often are you paid? _____

When do you get your paychecks? _____

What is your take-home pay? _____

What hours do you work? _____

UNION MEMBERSHIP

Are you a member of a union? _____

What is the union and the number of the local? _____

Do they have a credit union? _____

What is the name of the credit union? _____

What is the address of the credit union? _____

Do you have a savings account with the credit union? _____

How much is in the account? _____

What is the account number? _____

Do you have a loan with the credit union? _____

How much is the loan for? _____

What is the reason for the loan? _____

COMMISSIONS

Do you receive any employment commissions? _____

Bonuses or incentives? _____

How much do you get? _____

When do you get them? _____

OTHER EMPLOYMENT

Do you have another job? _____

It it part-time or full-time? _____

Where do you work? _____

What do you do? _____

What is the address? _____

A Private Eye's Guide

How many hours do you work each week? _____
How much are you paid? _____
What hours do you work? _____
How often are you paid? _____
When are you paid? _____
How much is your gross pay? _____
What is the name of the company or person who pays you?

_____
What is their address? _____
Do you have any other jobs? _____

FUTURE EMPLOYMENT
Do you have a contract, verbal or written, for future employment?

Who is the contract with? _____
What is your salary? _____
When do you start? _____
Are there any other benefits, compensations or bonuses?

_____

BUSINESS INCOME
Are you engaged in any type of business or self-employment?
If so, what kind? _____
What is the name and address of your business? _____
Did you start the business or purchase it? _____
If it was purchased, how much did you pay for it? _____
Who was it purchased from? _____
How long ago was it started or acquired? _____
Is the business a sole-ownership, partnership or corporation?
Is it listed as a Fictitious Business name with the County Clerk's office? _____
What name is it listed under? _____
Is it listed with any professional organizations or the secretary of state? _____

Under what name? _____

What hours do you work? _____

How many employees do you have? _____

How often are they paid? _____

When are they paid? _____

What is the weekly payroll? _____

What did you gross last year? _____

What did you net last year? _____

What bank is the account in? _____

Branch? _____

Account number? _____

Who owns the property where your business is located? __

Who do you pay your office rent to? _____

How much is the rent? _____

What day is it due? _____

What account do you pay it out of? _____

What is the security deposit? _____

PARTNERSHIPS

Do you have access to any business account for which you are authorized to sign? _____

What is the name of the business? _____

Address? _____

What bank is the account drawn on? _____

What branch is the account at? _____

What is the account number? _____

ACCOUNTANT

What is the name of your accountant? _____

How long has he or she been working for you? _____

What is his address? _____

Who was your accountant before that? _____

Who does your income tax returns? _____

What is his address? _____

How long has he done your tax returns? _____

Who did your tax returns before that? _____

MOTOR VEHICLES

Do you or your spouse own any automobiles? _____
How many? _____

CAR NUMBER ONE
What is the make and model of the car? _____
What is the color of the car? _____
What state is it registered in? _____
What is the plate number? _____
Who is the registered owner? _____
Who is the legal owner? _____
How much is the car worth? _____
How much money is still owed on the car? _____
Do you drive this car to work? _____
Where is the car kept? _____

CAR NUMBER TWO
What is the make and model of the car? _____
What color is the car? _____
What state is it registered in? _____
What is the plate number? _____
Who is the registered owner? _____
Who is the legal owner? _____
How much is the car worth? _____
How much is still owed on the car? _____
Do you drive this car to work? _____
Where is the car kept? _____

OTHER VEHICLES
Do you own any recreational vehicles, boats or airplanes? __
If so, how much did they cost? _____
When did you buy them? _____
Do you still owe anything on them? _____
How much? _____

194

Who do you owe the money to? _____

What is their address? _____

BANK ACCOUNTS

CHECKING ACCOUNTS

Do you or your spouse have any checking accounts? _____

How many? _____

ACCOUNT NUMBER ONE

What is the name on the account? _____

Is it a joint account? _____

What is the other name on the account? _____

Is it a personal or business account? _____

What bank is the account with? _____

Which branch? _____

What is the account number? _____

What is the balance of the account? _____

ACCOUNT NUMBER TWO

What is the name on the account? _____

Is it a joint account? _____

What is the other name on the account? _____

Is it a personal or business account? _____

What bank is the account with? _____

Which branch? _____

What is the account number? _____

What is the balance of the account? _____

OTHER ACCOUNTS

Do you have any other checking accounts, either held separately
or jointly? _____

Are there any other bank accounts you are authorized to sign on?

Do you have a check book on you? _____

What bank is it drawn on? _____

What is the balance? _____

What name is the account under? _____

SAVINGS ACCOUNTS

Do you have any savings accounts, held jointly or separately?

Whose names are they under? _____

What bank and branch are they located in? _____

What are the account numbers? _____

What are the balances on the account? _____

SAFETY DEPOSIT BOXES

Do you or your spouse have any safety deposit boxes? ____

What bank and branch is it located? _____

What is the box number? _____

What is in the box? _____

Is there any jewelry or personal property in the box? _____

SAVINGS BONDS

Do you or your spouse have any savings bonds? _____

What kind are they? _____

How much are they worth? _____

When were they purchased? _____

CASH

Do you have any cash on you right now? _____

(Take it! Your judgment allows you to do this!)

STOCKS

Do you or your spouse own any stock? _____

Whose name is it in? _____

How much are they worth? _____

Do you hold them in your possession? _____

If not, who does? _____

What is their address? _____

JUDGMENTS

Do you or your spouse hold a judgment against another party?

_____

Does anyone owe you a debt of any kind? _____

What is the name of the debtor? _____

What is their address? _____

How much is the debt for? _____

PERSONAL PROPERTY

Do you or your spouse own a watch, diamonds, or any other jewelry or antiques valued over $50.00? _____

What is it? _____

What is the value? _____

Where is it kept? _____

Do you or your spouse own a stamp collection? _____

A coin collection? _____

What is the value? _____

Where is it kept? _____

Do you or your spouse have any property in pawn right now?

What is it? _____

How much did you borrow against it? _____

When are you to redeem it? _____

Where is the pawn shop? _____

Do you own a TV set? _____

What brand is it? _____

What size screen does it have? _____

How much is it worth? _____

Do you own a VCR? _____

Is it VHS or Beta? _____

What brand is it? _____

Do you own any art? _____

Describe it. _____

Do you have any pets? _____

What kind are they? _____

TRUST FUNDS

Are you due any money from an estate? _____

Whose estate? _____

Where is the estate located? _____

What amount are you to receive? _____

When is the probate due to close? _____

Have you or your spouse ever inherited any money or property?

_____

From whom? _____

When did you inherit it? _____

How much did you inherit? _____

What did you do with the money? _____

Are you the beneficiary in any will? _____

Whose? _____

What relation are they to you? _____

What is their address? _____

Are you the beneficiary in any life insurance policies? ____

Whose? _____

What is their address? _____

How much is the policy for? _____

PROMISSORY NOTES

Have you received any time payments in the past five years?

When? _____

How much were they for? _____

What was done with the money? _____

Do you receive any increment payments as a result of property sales? _____

How much do you receive per month? _____

From whom? _____

What is their address? _____

How much was the loan for? _____

What is the balance due? _____

Is there a balloon payment? _____

Where is the money deposited? _____

Do you receive any other money on a regular basis? _____

Quarterly? _____

Annual? _____

BENEFITS

Have you ever been injured in an accident of any kind? __

Did you sue the responsible party? _____

Did you receive any compensation? _____

Is there a suit still pending? _____

Name of the suit? _____

What county is it filed in? _____

TAX REFUNDS

Did you get a federal or state income tax refund last year?

How much was it for? _____

What did you do with the money? _____

Do you anticipate getting one this year? _____

COPYRIGHTS, ETC.

Have you filed a copyright, trade name certificate or partnership certificate in the last five years? _____

If so, please detail the transaction. _____

Has a license or permit been granted to you by any governmental agency? _____

Are you acting as the guardian, trustee or in any other capacity under any will, agreement or appointment? _____

If so, explain. _____

Now...

1.   If you haven't already done so, ask your debtor to hand over whatever cash he or she has in his pockets. (Your judgment entitles you to do this.) 2.

2.   Record any abstract judgments in any counties where the scoundrel has property.

3.   Investigate all real property to see if there is enough equity to consider forcing a sale.

4.   Send writs of attachment to; Anyone renting property from your scoundrel, anyone who owes him money, the telephone company (if the bill is in his name), his landlord (if he rents his apartment or office and has a security deposit,) to anyone who owes the scoundrel money via a promissory note, anyone who owes him money via a judgment, the attorney handling any trust fund where he is getting or anticipating an inheritance, any banks where he has a checking account, savings account, safety deposit box or savings bonds, any brokerage firm holding stocks, the sherrif, making a demand on any personal property not exempted by law.

5.   Garnish his wages, if he has a job.

6.   Put a till on any appropriate businesses.

7.   Subpoena his income tax returns from his accountant. (You cannot subpoena information from the IRS. You can, however, subpoena any information regarding your judgment from his accountant. This includes his federal and state income tax returns!)

8.   Follow up on any cars to see if there is enough equity to warrant attaching them. (You should have all the information you need, including where to find them at home or work, and the hours they will be there.)

Good luck!

Index

Related Books

Everybody's Guide to Small Claims Court by Attorney Ralph Warner. Step-by-step instructions on how to initiate or defend a small claims case, with state-by-state information. 304 pages, **$15.95**

The Independent Paralegal's Handbook by Ralph Warner. Legal and practical guidelines for preparing bankruptcy, divorce, incorporation, landlord-tenant & probate papers. 300 pages, **$19.95**

Money Troubles: Legal Strategies to Cope with Your Debts by Attorney Robin Leonard. How to obtain your credit report, challenge wage attachments & handle bill collectors - plus information on credit, loans, secured & unsecured debts, taxes, alimony, child support, bankruptcy, becoming judgment-proof, what to expect if sued, and how to start over after a financial setback. 350 pages, **$16.95**

Public Records Primer - 3rd California Edition by Don Ray. A guide to information kept by the state, city, county and federal governments in California - plus library and newspaper information. Great for librarians, reporters & investigators. 150 pages, **$14.95**

How to Understand & Buy Computers by Dan Gookin. This in-depth book tells how computers work in simple, understandable terms. 200 pages, **$8.95**

The CreditPower Handbook for American Consumers by Professor Dan Berman. A step-by-step guide containing the identical information credit repair clinics charge up to $800 for! 204 pages, **$14.95**

You Can Find Anyone by Eugene Ferraro. The in's and out's of finding old friends, lovers and deadbeats. 144 pages, **$14.95**

Collect Your Court Judgment by Scott, Elias & Goldoftas. Locate debtors and their assets, plus step-by-step instructions & forms for getting your money. For help in collecting judgments when assets or debtors are located in California. 464 pages, **$24.95**

The Handbook on Child Support Enforcement by the U.S. Government Printing Office. How to apply for child support enforcement services, finding the absent parent, establishing paternity, getting and enforcing the support order and working across state lines. 47 pages, **$4.95**

The Check is Not in the Mail by Leonard Sklar. If cash-flow is your problem, invest in this book. It's cheaper than attending a credit-managing seminar or writing off a lot of bad debts. 289 pages, **$19.95**

County Courthouse Book by Elizabeth Petty Bentley. Lists America's 3,351 county courthouses, addresses and phone numbers, plus the types of records available. 386 pages, **$29.95**

International Vital Records Handbook by Thomas Kemp. Where to write worldwide for birth, death and marriage records. 355 pages, **$24.95**

The Instant National Locator Guide by Fay Faron Find over 8,100 U.S. cities and towns *Fast* in this one-stop directory & atlas (With a IBM compatable disk of your region, the cost is $50 - call (415) 922-6684 for details.) 320 pages, **Book Only: $15.95**

Creighton-Morgan Publishing
P.O. Box 470862
San Francisco   CA   94147-0862
(415)   922-6684

SALES ORDER № PEYEG

DATE:

SEND TO:

NAME

ADDRESSS

PHONE   EXT.

✓ TERMS: PAY WITH ORDER, CHECK OR MONEY ORDER

QTY	DESCRIPTION	UNIT PRICE	AMOUNT
	Thank You		
	SUBTOTAL		
TAX, CALIFORNIA RESIDENTS ONLY: 7%			
SHIPPING & HANDLING, 1ST ORDER			$3 50
EACH ADDITIONAL ORDER		$1 00	
RECEIVED BY		TOTAL	